PORKIES WILDERNESS WANDERINGS

Outdoors Adventures and Wanderings
in the Porcupine Mountains
Wilderness State Park

John Highlen

NATURAL CONNECTIONS
Deerton, Michigan

Copyright © 2022 John Highlen
All rights reserved
First Edition

Published by Natural Connections 2022

ISBN 978-1-7338916-2-2 (paperback)

Printed in the United States of America

A portion of the story "Artist-in-Residence" first appeared in Marquette Monthly Magazine

ALSO BY JOHN HIGHLEN

Touching the Wild U.P.

To the *Friends of the Porkies*, for all of the dreams they help bring to life.

The Porkies—It's not just a park in the Upper Peninsula. It's the Upper Peninsula in a Park.

Contents

Acknowledgements...9
Introduction...13

Artist-in-Residence..17
Presque Isle Falls..25
Nonesuch...33
Venturing Out..39
Hemlocks...43
Flowing..47
Nonesuch Trout...51
Bugs...55
Union River Fishing..59
Little Carp Trout..65
Union River Visions..71
Seasons..75
Rained-Out Plans...81
Trap Falls..85
Transition..91
Paddling Lake of the Clouds...95
West Escarpment...103
Evening Stroll...111
Wanderings...115
Walking Into Winter...123
Views..129
Wish List...133
Parting Thoughts...137

ACKNOWLEDGEMENTS

A special thank-you to my wife, Julie, for initiating this book project by inviting me to participate in her artist-in-residence adventure. I am also indebted to her for helping bring this project to completion with her eye-catching watercolor painting for the cover and artwork to enhance each chapter.

I very much appreciate our friend, Barb Osbon, for applying her proofreading talents to this book. She was politely diligent in pointing out all of those things that I have forgotten from my high school and college English classes.

Thank-you to the *Friends of the Porkies* for their dedication to the park and for sponsoring the Artist-in-Residence program. I especially appreciate their vision for creating Dan's Cabin for the artists' stay. It's an incredible gift! My *Friends of the Porkies* acknowledgements would not be complete without thanking Sherrie McCabe, who cheerfully and tirelessly facilitates the artist program for the Friends Group. She is now not only a Friend of the Porkies, but a friend of ours.

The Porcupine Mountains Wilderness State Park staff are also due a big thank-you. I've always found them to be pleasantly helpful. Park Interpreter, Katie Urban, is certainly no exception. Her enthusiastic help and guidance enriched our Porkies experiences.

Most importantly, I thank God for the gift of the Porkies and all of those adventures that made this book a reality.

PORKIES INTRODUCTION

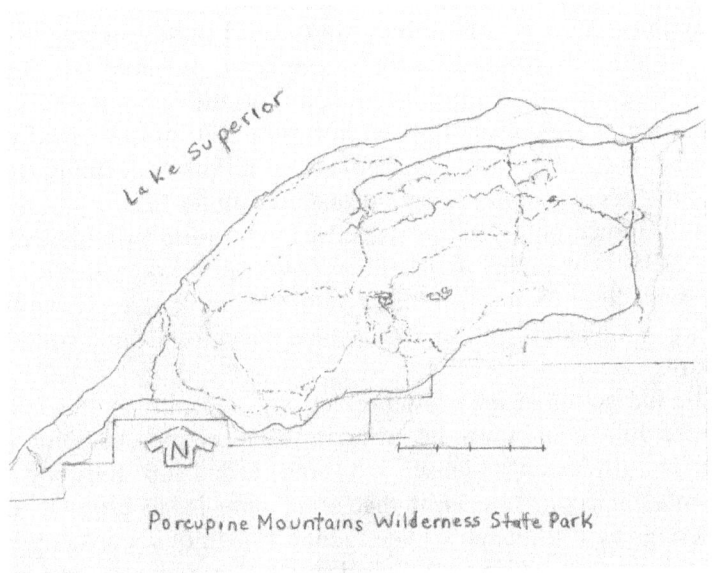

Porcupine Mountains Wilderness State Park

I vaguely remember visiting the Porkies for the first time on a family vacation when I was a kid. I'd have to try to dig out an old photograph to even be able to guess how old I was at the time. That trip was followed by a short backpacking venture with my dad when I was in high school. College days at Michigan Tech included a couple of multi-day backcountry ski-touring adventures with my friend Bill.

All of those visits were fun and adventurous, but they were simply stand-alone excursions with no real connection being made. I didn't really begin to get acquainted with the park until my wife, Julie, was an artist-in-residence with the Friends of the Porkies in

January of 2020. Spending two weeks living in the park at Dan's Cabin, when relatively few other people were around to bump into, was like having a serious date with someone you've known on a casual basis for a number of years. I wasn't sure what to expect, but in the back of my mind, I was figuring it would probably just be an enjoyable time with no long-term ramifications.

By the second day of our two-week stay, I started laying plans to apply for an artist-in-residence of my own to more thoroughly explore and write during the autumn parade of colors. After submitting the application, I wasn't sure if I would actually be selected, but just in case, I made plans for a Porkies camping trip in May in order to sample springtime and prepare for fall.

As it turned out, I did get selected for an artist-in-residence, but then COVID stormed in, shutting down the park and stranding everyone closer to home. I didn't get to do any Porkies spring trout fishing or kayaking, but my dreams and plans for autumn continued to grow.

We did get to spend a few Porkies days camping in August that year, so Julie could make her artist-in-residence presentation. With COVID still on the loose, we both ended up fulfilling our presentation commitments at that same time in an effort to keep gatherings to a minimum. Even though I had not yet actually been an artist-in-residence myself, I had done a considerable amount of writing during Julie's residency, so I had plenty of experience to talk about. I also managed to squeeze in a couple of fly fishing forays and a wet hike during that August stay, just to pack as much into that trip as we could.

The long-awaited October artist-in-residence visit in 2020 was a two-and-a-half-week immersion that included paddling Lake of the Clouds in our canoe. We also got to sample pretty much the entire range of weather conditions, just to make the experience complete.

The next spring, we had the same plans as the previous year, just a different May. Those 2020 plans finally came to fruition in 2021 —more or less.

Somewhere in that mix of winter, summer, fall, and spring adventures, a connection was forged. Actually, it was more than a connection. It was a commitment. There's a bond now in place. A relationship.

PORKIES WILDERNESS WANDERINGS

This book is a chronicle of sorts. A collection of wanderings and thoughts in and about the Porcupine Mountains Wilderness State Park. A place friends simply refer to as *The Porkies*.

John Highlen
January 2022
Deerton, Michigan

ARTIST-IN-RESIDENCE

A few January snowflakes drifted down as we loaded our six-foot sled with a couple of weeks-worth of food and supplies. My wife, Julie, had the privilege of being artist-in-residence in the Porkies, to portray the park in a series of acrylic paintings. She was preparing for the roughly two-mile trek into Dan's Cabin, which was built by the *Friends of the Porkies* in memory of Dan Urbanski, a local nature photographer. Being the support crew, I got to pull the sled. We both carried day-packs stuffed with gear as well. A bigger pack and three large duffels of gear would come in on the second trip. Our host, Sherrie McCabe, who leads the artist program for the Porkies Friends group, and her friend Melissa Santini, led the way as we embarked on our two-week adventure.

The Artist-in-Residence cabin is nestled in a quiet stand of mature hemlocks near the Little Union River. Even though it's rustic, meaning no electricity or indoor plumbing, we found the accommodations extremely comfortable and relaxing. After getting our introduction to the cabin, we quickly unloaded and headed out for the rest of our supplies. The last of our gear was unloaded and stowed away as darkness began filling the cabin. The flickering glow of a soy candle provided the feel of warmth as we built a fire in the woodstove for the real thing. The antique Charm No. 23, as it stated on the ornate cast-iron door, was aptly named as it did indeed work like a charm, readily warming the cabin. So, with a slight freezing drizzle falling outside, we settled into our first evening of candle-light and wood heat and began laying plans for our first full day in the park before turning in for the night.

As the official artist, Julie slept in the log-frame twin bed tucked into its own bedroom corner. I took the fold-out bed in the main living area, situated beneath two large picture windows, giving me a view of the night sky beyond the tops of neighboring hemlocks and maples. I enjoyed the feel of sleeping out under the stars without snow falling in my face. I remember watching from my sleeping bag one night as clouds rolled past the half-moon like billows of campfire smoke. There was another night that I witnessed the full-moon creating rainbow halos in a veil of thin clouds. Most mornings I awoke to a gallery of frosty artwork decorating my windows to the world.

Why did Julie choose January to spend two weeks living out in the woods in the Porkies? Well, in her own words, "I hoped to hear what is thought to be silent, see the rainbow of color in what is thought to be white, and feel warmth in what is thought to be cold. To capture the magic of mature woods in winter on canvas that causes the viewer to stop and feel the comfort the blanket of snow provides, despite the frost in the air."

So, from a cozy cabin near a cascading waterfall in the forest, we set out to do just that.

Our typical day started with a fire to warm cabin and spirits, followed by breakfast of oatmeal with nuts, dried fruit and home-made maple syrup. By mid-morning, with the day's plans in mind, we would leave cabin comforts behind and immerse ourselves in the winter woods, traversing new trails, snowshoeing along meandering streams, and exploring the surrounding forest. Most of our wanderings were limited to the park's east side due to snow conditions, our limited means of travel, and because Julie stopped often to study scenes and capture reference pictures in order to accomplish her painting goals.

The exception was the day we decided to hike out to our vehicle and make the drive over to the park's west side to explore the Presque Isle River falls area. We debated if the drive was worth doing until we stepped out of our car in the midst of a shadowed hemlock forest heavily pocked by deer tracks, with the snow-muffled music of rushing water calling through the trees. Our entire afternoon was spent exploring down the west side of the river, out along Superior, then back up the river's east side, building a collection of photographs, notes, and memories.

Other adventures and wanderings included Union Spring, Little Union River gorge, Nonesuch Falls, and many of the eastern rivers. We also snowshoed to the east and west vistas near the ski hill, viewing Superior to the east and the escarpment disappearing into a snowy mist to the west.

Because we chose to primarily use the Outpost Campground latrine that was roughly a quarter-mile away instead of the composter at the cabin, even nighttime trips to the outhouse, with the moon shining through the trees creating vivid shadows clawing at the snowy ground, turned into adventures.

On Saturday, we decided to participate in some park activities because Julie, as artist-in-residence, wanted opportunities to interact with more people than we had been seeing during our usual ventures. So early afternoon, we joined a guided snowshoe hike led by Park Interpreter Katie Urban. That was when we visited the East Vista by riding the chairlift to the top of the ski hill, then snowshoeing over to the vista and down around the mountain.

That evening, we enjoyed a lantern-lit trail hike near Superior, also hosted by Katie. Both adventures were interesting and enjoyable ways to meet new people as we experienced new perspectives of the park.

Throughout our adventures, it seemed like every day we thought we were thoroughly covering the eastern area of the park, but every time we looked, we found something new.

Though explorations and picture taking went well, actually painting turned out to be a little less productive than Julie originally anticipated. She had successfully done some winter plein air painting in the past, but conditions didn't cooperate so well during her residency. Most days were overcast with light snow, which are certainly not ideal conditions for painting. One sunny day, it felt comfortable outside, so Julie set up her easel near the cabin, intent on painting a tiny creek meandering through the hemlocks. The sunshine proved to be misleading, though, as the actual temperature was still only twenty-four degrees Fahrenheit, so brush-cleaning water and paint still wanted to freeze fairly quickly. Evenings in the cabin, candle and lantern light were inadequate for mixing and properly matching colors. So actual artwork accomplishments during the residency were limited to a few pencil sketches, several small watercolor studies and a few small acrylic paintings. However, Julie did successfully assemble a collection of nearly a thousand reference photographs.

The residency came to a close in the middle of a two-day snowstorm, making for a memorable trek out with all of our gear. In a way, it felt strange to be leaving. Dan's Cabin had become "home" and we had looked forward to returning there each evening. The two weeks that sounded so long at the beginning had passed surprisingly quickly. We were amazed at how rapidly our idea of "normal" had changed and how things that were thought to be necessities soon faded to minor conveniences.

Our adventures had been numerous: watching a fisher through the cabin window, witnessing the transition of rushing water to its state of suspended animation, reading stories of otters written in snow along with tales of snowshoe hares, deer, pine squirrels, beavers, and grouse. Through the seemingly silent winter woods we had listened to the songs of streams changing with the season, the north wind giving voice to the hemlocks, and whispers of snowflakes coming to rest. Endless white had revealed shadows of blue and lavender, gleaming silver highlights, and warm amber hues ebbing across the snowscape as the sun tracked across the sky.

PORKIES WILDERNESS WANDERINGS

Julie's artist-in-residence may have been done, but the Porkies paintings and our relationship with the park had just begun. With sixty-thousand acres in the park, including forty-two-thousand acres of wilderness, I knew there was still much exploring left to enjoy. That's why, during our time there, I had written an application of my own for an opportunity to return in the fall. Somewhat to my surprise, I was blessed with an acceptance.

In October, we came back to the park to live simply, explore, and nurture our growing friendship with the Porkies. With Julie's artist-in-residence only a handful of months in the past, that time in the park and life at Dan's Cabin were still vivid memories. So when we first opened the door at the beginning of my residency and were greeted by the familiar subtle mingling scents of raw wood and aged woodsmoke, it felt like a welcome home. Like we had just been away for a day of wanderings and were returning for our evening meal. Mentally, I was already settled in as I stepped through the doorway.

Early on, we reveled in the warmth of autumn colors. A few days later, it was thirtyish and snowing. There were six inches on the ground in the cabin area. More over around Mirror Lake. At first, the snow was an interesting autumn novelty. But after more than a week of autumn snow, I began wrestling with the idea that it might be more than just a novelty. During lunch one day, a couple of avalanches came off the roof. I went out and took a few pictures of our canoe sitting upside-down near the cabin, covered in snow. That morning, I shoveled the cabin walkway. Ninety minutes later, I cleaned off at least another inch, as more collected on the bill of my Stormy Kromer.

I've found that on a relatively long wilderness venture, it usually starts out hectic, trying to squeeze in as much as possible. After a few days, it typically transitions into a sense of relaxing, feeling like you have plenty of time to roam. Then, as time winds down, it picks up speed again and a new sense of urgency emerges. No matter the pace of the day, though, we spent our time in the park steeping ourselves in the varying moods and moments of autumn. When you're here for an extended time, this becomes the focus of life. Living in the moment becomes easier. Distractions are just the basics of life, like eating, sleeping, staying warm and keeping clean.

They become part of the means, adding to the whole instead of detracting from it.

A longer visit in the Porkies, like an artist-in-residence or extended stay, allows time to do simple things we don't seem to find time for at home, where meals and dish washing, home and auto repairs, yardwork, careers, and television rule our to-do lists.

You have time for following a stream to see where it goes and what it's up to. Read the tales of other visitors in sand and mud and snow. Search out lairs of skittish trout and turn over rocks to see who lives in the neighborhood. Study the stream's flow, discerning causes for its patterns. Study stones. Appreciate sand patterns. Notice forests of moss on a rock. Patterns of ice crystals on quiet pools and backwaters.

You can work on distinguishing trees by their skeleton shapes and bark patterns, pondering why they're growing where they're growing. Or, imagine tales of the land told by its geographic features.

You can read a book by your favorite outdoors author, or maybe a potential new favorite. Read that poetry you look at on your shelf, but never seem to find the time for at home. Read your bible, especially if you've never really read it before.

Read the tale of eternity in the night sky. Marvel at how all of the little pieces of creation fit exactly together in the whole of the world around you.

Trace your path to the present, and chart your way forward.

Greet the first soft glimmerings of a new day creeping across the landscape with a quiet cup of tea, feeling the rotation of the earth into the sun. Then, ponder the day's events as the great sphere you're riding continues to spin, pulling the last rays of light over the cusp of the horizon.

Record the details of life as it unfolds, capturing its musings and miracles on paper or canvas.

Through experiences like this, I have learned to take opportunities as they come, because opportunities are difficult to plan for.

Once again, two weeks sounded like a long time when I was planning, but I was surprised at how quickly the first week passed by. Somehow, the second week disappeared even quicker, and there

PORKIES WILDERNESS WANDERINGS

I was, on my last full day, writing a note in the cabin log book to those who would share my connection with Dan's Cabin.

That place had been the focal point of life for the past two weeks. The hub of all of our wanderings and explorations. Our weather had been just what you would predict for mid-October in the western Upper Peninsula, unpredictable. Warmth and sunshine, cold and clouds, brilliant colors and a thick blanket of snow had greeted us on any given day. We had experienced the many faces and moods of the park's wilderness, hiking a hundred and twenty-five miles by my calculations, including portaging our canoe into Lake of the Clouds—and back out—twice, to experience the lake and its feeding river on a more personal level than a bird's-eye view.

Through all of these wanderings, I'm sure I still don't know the park as well as some, but probably better than most. Of all the experiences we enjoyed in the Porkies, one of my favorites was Dan's Cabin. That had been the center of our world for more than a month during the course of the year. A welcoming comfort at the end of each adventurous day. A place for a warm meal, relaxing evening, and refreshing sleep. Porkies memories and Dan's Cabin run together and complement each other in my mind.

The cabin itself is a wood-lovers home. It has a basic, simple construction, with just enough flair to be interesting without looking fancy or gaudy. The peak window, a couple of curved supports, and antique woodstove elevate Dan's Cabin a step above a regular old cabin. Even before we packed up and left, I was already beginning to feel a loss for having to leave.

In a way, I almost felt more comfortable there than at our own cabin. It's just an extremely comfortable and inviting place. I liked hearing the Little Union River cascading by whenever I stepped outside. I liked looking at the hemlocks and maples out the windows. I liked the sheltered entries with porches protecting against the elements. I loved lying in bed at night, looking out the big windows at the night sky and nearby tree silhouettes. I appreciated the efficiency and warmth of the old woodstove with flames releasing the sun's stored-up energy from days long past. I loved the wood construction made from local trees. I loved the scent of the cabin when I walked through the door. I loved being there long enough to settle in instead of feeling like I was just stopping by.

I loved sitting in the old oak rocking chair with a cup of tea or coffee, thinking things over, or sometimes just sipping and being there. I loved working at the wooden table and being able to stare out into the forest as I searched for the right words.

I've been blessed to experience a number of north woods cabins, but Dan's Cabin will always stand out in my mind and make me yearn for those days of exploring, experiencing, and simply living there in the Porkies. I don't know if I will ever be able to return to Dan's Cabin, but part of me will always be there anyway.

Besides a collection of adventures, pictures, and memories—in addition to assembling a mass of notes—what emerged from my artist-in-residence experience was a head full of dreams and plans. The more adventures I have in the Porkies, the more I've come to realize that this relationship is still just beginning. There's no doubt that the kid in me will never tire of that sixty-thousand-acre playground.

Presque Isle Falls

The January morning started out with a thermometer reading of eleven degrees Fahrenheit. Our plan was to explore the Presque Isle River Falls area, which with the winter closure of South Boundary Road, isn't an easy thing to do from the east side of the park. It involved nearly a 149-mile round trip, by way of Wakefield and Route 519. We parked where the county road meets up with the west end of South Boundary Road, which is where road-plowing ends. Other than a couple of trucks attached to empty snowmobile trailers, we were the only ones there.

The afternoon venture was my wife, Julie's, idea. Having never seen Presque Isle Falls in person before, I had been debating whether or not it was worth the long drive. Being the official artist-in-residence for the January visit, Julie won the debate.

As we strapped on our snowshoes and headed out, following the sound of falling water through towering hemlocks, I was glad I hadn't won the debate, but it seemed a little too early to actually admit it out loud. So I quietly shuffled along, scanning all around for the makers of the deer trails that crisscrossed the forest. We spotted six does, but based on the number of tracks and trails, I was expecting to see more like thirty.

We use traditional wood-frame snowshoes because we prefer their quietness and aesthetics, but, negotiating some of the steep hills near the river, I found myself liking the idea of the built-in traction claws of the modern metal-frame designs. It's not the sliding down the hill on snowshoes that's the problem. The problem comes at the end of the descent, when your snowshoes disappear under a considerable amount of snow just as you're trying to lift your foot for the next step to accommodate the downhill momentum of your body. Snowshoe claws would certainly help keep you from sliding into that predicament. As I recall, neither of us actually fell, but there were definitely a few less-than-graceful moments.

Along the river, we found a collection of otter tracks, but were disappointed that we didn't see the playful track-maker. One of the great things about winter is that you can read the stories written in snow, even though you may have missed the live performance. Tracks in the snow, evidence of unseen dramas, give witness to stories that go untold in other seasons.

The three named falls—Nawadaha, Manido, and Manabezho—were separated by a collection of rapids and cascades, some of which I thought were deserving of names of their own. Then again, maybe their anonymity is part of their charm.

Below the last falls is a final rushing caldron, before the Presque Isle's peaceful and graceful entrance into Superior. That rushing torrent is along the west side of the roughly three-acre almost-an-island that likely gives Presque Isle its name. On the east side of the shaded hemlock, red pine and aspen almost-island resides a quiet lagoon. Based on the sculpted Nonesuch shale features at the upper end of the lagoon and the old logjam of once-upon-a-time trees at the lower end, it appeared that the tranquil lagoon is itself sometimes part of the Presque Isle River's flow.

As we approached the suspension bridge across the river, a large whitetail doe foraging on the far bank was spotlighted by the afternoon sun. We quietly watched from the forest shadows as she slowly worked her way up through a thin patch of brightly lit aspens to the shelter of the hemlocks above.

At Superior, telltale tracks betrayed the passing of a small pack of coyotes as they traversed the arctic-looking landscape. Wave-splashed icy snow mounds glistened along the shoreline in the afternoon sun. Within a few minutes, clouds moved in, blocking out the cheery glow, leaving the world in cold white. Plumes of Superior erupted through a blow-hole in one of the icy mounds each time a wave rolled in.

Looking eastward, down some twenty-six miles of Superior wilderness shoreline, I thought about how much exploring there was still to do in the park. I knew those explorations wouldn't be right then, but I began to wonder when. Vague plans began to formulate as I stared into the distance. Another artist-in-residence, perhaps? A cross-park adventure on foot, or maybe a venture down the length of the shoreline by kayak? I often find that when I'm exploring, especially in areas that are new to me, there are ideas lurking about, waiting to be fed, fostered, and turned loose to become new adventures.

We followed the east-side trail back upstream, through a deer-tracked hemlock forest, accented here and there with cedars and maples. Anywhere a cedar was down, deer had eaten it to a skeleton. One cedar had split and fallen over with the trunk still held a few feet above the ground. That skeleton had a mohawk-strip of green along the top, just beyond a deer's reach. Another cedar was at the river's edge, with a heavy deer trail down a steep treacherous hill to reach it. I wondered how the deer had even found that dining opportunity in the first place. I didn't notice any other reason for them to trek down there, but somehow they knew.

Not much farther upstream, I came across a deer bed next to an old hemlock, right at the brink of a steep drop-off to the river, overlooking Manido Falls. I admired the deer's choice of location and wondered if it had anything to do with the scenery or if it was simply a good tactical vantage point to keep an eye out for potential threats while resting.

Nearby, a well-used deer trail crossed the river in a swift, shallow stretch, where tannin waters flowed over layers of Nonesuch shale. Most people, even accomplished waders, would likely struggle to cross the river there due to swift water and potentially slippery footing. Deer, however, not hindered with thoughts of doom in these wild conditions, apparently crossed the Presque Isle there on a regular basis.

A little farther upstream, just below Nawadaha Falls, there was a twelve-inch diameter slab of Nonesuch shale hanging from the frost-covered cliff. The slab's precarious position appeared to only be supported by a small patch of frozen shale fragments. I suspected that a twenty-foot plunge was imminent. An icicle hanging from the lower edge of the dangling slab was likely working to hasten the fall.

As we neared the end of our loop of the Presque Isle Falls area, I spent some time reflecting on our experience. Overall, I felt that even though the east-side trail lacked fancy stairs and boardwalks, it provided some of the best winter views of the falls—both named and unnamed. Both sides of the river held masses of deer tracks, but the six deer we had spotted early on were our only wildlife sightings of the afternoon, which was actually a good thing due to the fact that it's not good to disturb deer when they're yarded-up because it causes them to unnecessarily burn energy to avoid the human intrusion.

Our brief stand-still brought on a chill, which shouldn't have been surprising with the temperature riding around the eighteen-degree mark. Still, we were plenty warm while walking, so I hadn't expected to get chilled so quickly. The afternoon was waning, and a fire was sounding better by the minute, so we decided to head back to the cabin.

I thought about that adventure as we traversed the Presque Isle Falls loop again in October. The sky looked about the same as it had in January as we stepped into the woods near the main parking area. We weren't sure if the dismal look of the sky was due to impending snow or rain. Either way, it didn't look promising.

PORKIES WILDERNESS WANDERINGS

As is often the case in upper Michigan, the weather changed abruptly as we approached the river. The sun broke through, igniting the grove of sugar maples we were in. The illuminated amber mix of sugar maples and yellow birches made me seriously think about getting out my sunglasses. Though much of the park—even much of the Upper Peninsula for that matter—was barren of leaves, autumn color was in full swing there near the Presque Isle River. In fact, I would have called it *peak* color. The brightness even extended into the hemlocks and cedars that dominated the strip of land right along the riverbank.

The river was running a little murky—even beyond the normal tannin coloring—due to recent rains. With a little added flow, the water was churning wildly. Just above the suspension foot-bridge, a half-bowl was being scoured out of the shale formation on the east side of the river by an aggressive swirl of water. The sides of the bowl were as smooth as if they were being finished by extra-fine wet sandpaper. It was polished to a glistening shine.

We had headed over to the Presque Isle expecting to be greeted by a crowd, but were happy to find that we were wrong. There were other people, but I certainly wouldn't have called it crowded. We figured that the lack of color elsewhere had kept them at bay. Whatever the reason, it was our good fortune.

The suspension bridge bounced with each step. Julie had to wait for everyone else to get off before she could even take an unblurred picture of the river. I didn't remember that being an issue back in January, but then again, we were the only ones there in January, so we didn't have other people bouncing and swaying the bridge.

I stood at the southern tip of the almost-island, looking into the churning river. Raw hydraulic power was working up a froth. I have respect for the Presque Isle, much like the Tahquamenon. Both are beautiful and inspiring, but deserving of caution and respect. As a sign along the Presque Isle notes, a slip could prematurely end your vacation.

Besides the three named falls in that section of the river, I found myself drawn to even the minor "falls" where the river spills over only a few layers of Nonesuch shale. I thought that any of those little plunges or cascades would be worthy of a name, although it would be a monumental task to name each one, no matter how creative a person was. Part of their beauty is in the way they change with variations in flow, weather and lighting. I've come to consider the falls, cascades, and rapids of this lower stretch of the Presque Isle to rival any in the state. Those thin orange curtains of water sliding over shelves of shale create a masterpiece of river art. The shale itself, toned in grays and browns, overlaid with a myriad of patterns, is an artistic work as well.

We crossed the sculpted channel at the head of what is obviously at times part of the river's path around the east side of the almost-island. For the moment, it was dry ground, waiting for a spring surge to once again bring to it the flow of life. Climbing up into the hemlocks, the trail then took on a more distant river view. Near Manido Falls, not to be outdone by the main flow, a tiny feeder creek softly tumbled and gurgled down through layers of shale on its way to join the main show.

We found a large toad in the muddy trail, slowly walking instead of hopping. I was surprised to see it out so late in the season, especially with the cold spells we had recently experienced. We also came across one of the bent-over cedars we had visited in January. There was still only one green branch sticking up too high for deer to reach, but it appeared to be alive. Plants just don't know how to quit.

Near Nawadaha Falls, some hemlock and cedar trees were perched right on the brink of the cliff, curving out and up, still reaching for the life-giving sun. They were destined to become part of the woody debris in the river, or more likely, part of the collection of logs at the mouth. I remembered photographing one of those cedars in January—the one out at the nose of the cliff—with large icicles hanging from the cliff face. The tree had outlasted the icicles and was still boldly hanging onto life. I read that in Ojibwa, Nawadaha means, *In the midst of a rapids*. I also read that during spring runoff, twelve thousand gallons of water per second flows over those rapids and falls. We decided that we needed to return in spring to see that spectacle for ourselves.

Heading back toward the lake along the west side of the falls, we stopped near Manabezho, the lower falls, to admire a lone amber-orange maple that was casting a reflection out onto the river. Near it, a small straight section of rainbow reached out from the falls into the rising mist.

PORKIES WILDERNESS WANDERINGS

After completing our planned loop, we crossed the suspension bridge once again to explore along the Superior shoreline near the river mouth. Right where the river chokes down to its narrowest width, I discovered a lone purple lupine, still in full bloom, looking fresh and perky as it defied the season. Beyond was a scattered array of weathered logs and roots decorating the sand-and-cobble beach. It made me think of that cedar near Nawadaha Falls that, after another season, or maybe a few, would likely be joining the shoreline collection.

Four-foot whitecaps were rolling in, churning sand into the already-murky river water. A hundred-yard-wide band of brown water hugged the shore. Beyond the almost-island, there was no real beach. Superior waves were crashing directly into the edge of the shoreline forest. Trees were giving way, leaning into the advancing surf. In a way, I felt bad for those trees as I walked away, leaving them in their state of impending doom. Later, sitting in front of a crackling fire pondering the day's events, flowing tannin water, rolling Superior waves, and trees in varying states of life all fit nicely into the ever-changing whole of the world outside. People fit in there somewhere, too—not only as stewards and caretakers, but as participants in the ongoing drama.

I put another log on the fire and began thinking about my role in that grand scheme.

Nonesuch

The day felt cold for October. Temperature-wise it was hovering right near freezing, so it wasn't really that cold by UP standards. The sky was a cloudy blah, which wasn't uncommon. Maybe it was because of the dampness, or maybe the barometric pressure was doing something squirrely. Whatever it was, Julie and I both noticed it. We both felt a chill creeping in.

It was an easy day as far as hiking. We took our time eating breakfast and getting ready, not hitting the trail until mid-morning. Our focus was Nonesuch Falls and the mine site. That area had touched us for some reason when we had visited back in January, so we were anxious to return for more in-depth exploring. One of the things that certainly caught my attention on our previous visit was the way the Little Iron River was slowly crystallizing from the falls down through the old mine site. I could still vividly picture it in my mind, and I wanted to see if the recent cold weather had started the process again. Also, during our January visit, nobody else had been there in quite a while, so the snow was unmarred by human activity. That cold, untouched look gave the mine site an entrancing feel.

According to park signs, the mine had operated on-and-off from the 1860s through the early 1900s—roughly fifty years of operation. At its peak, it involved more than a hundred residents. Like many old mining and logging sites, it was basically a self-contained town, complete with apple trees and flower gardens.

During this October visit, we didn't see any of the exotic flowers that were rumored to be lingering around, but we did taste-test one of the apples we discovered on a tree at the edge of the old townsite. It wasn't the best wild-growing apple I ever tasted, but it wasn't bad, considering where it was growing. I thought it would've been better in a pie or crisp than eaten fresh off the tree, but based on the muddied area of deer tracks under the tree and three well-worn game trails connecting to it, I guessed that the local deer population would disagree with me on that thought.

Even though the Nonesuch mining venture wasn't considered to be a success, which was common in endeavors like that, it did supposedly spur the start-up of the White Pine Copper Mine a few miles to the east, which turned into one of the most profitable copper mines in the Upper Peninsula. From what I understand, the undoing of the Nonesuch mine was in its name. Nonesuch shale and sandstone, which gave the mine its name, contain very fine deposits of copper, like thin copper foil entrapped in the rock. The difficulty and expense of extracting copper from the Nonesuch sandstone became the venture's demise.

Now, the town and mine site, once bustling with activity and dreams, are silent collections of rubble with the Little Iron River still making its journey through. Nonesuch Falls, and the rapids below, are still singing background melody to anyone that will listen. I doubted that many of the miners or their families listened. To them, the river was likely nothing more than a resource to be used, like trees for wood. Depending on the noise and commotion of the mining operation, they may not have even been able to hear the river's voice, let alone listened.

Mining rubble still sits in heaps and piles overlooking the falls, with the river flowing through the edge of the tailings. Regardless of past or present happenings, the Little Iron flows on, just as it did before the miners arrived and as it has since they left. The river cares nothing of man's doings or desires. It simply continues with its intended task, carrying on toward Superior.

As I mentioned, back in January, we had witnessed the drama of the Little Iron slowly crystallizing, transforming into a collection of frozen works of art. Numerous shallow cascades and slicks contained ice formations in a multitude of shades of amber and white, formed from varying degrees of solidified river and snow. There were formations like half saucers full of tannin water. With some, water delicately trickled over the entire icy lip. With others, the ice rim protruded slightly above the water's surface, with the overflow rushing through one small area, like a breach in a beaver dam. Water, somewhere between liquid and ice, sluggishly slid over the lip. There were ice formations and semi-ice formations. Layered cascades, not truly frozen, more like water in suspended animation. More than slush, but not quite yet ice. Flow in limbo. Scalloped-edge tiers being formed by slushy water oozing out onto near-ice, creating these patterns. I just couldn't stop admiring them. They reminded me of delicate, freshly bloomed wildflowers that would only be in that state for but a relative moment. They looked like fine crystalline sculptures crafted by angelic beings. The formations reminded me of the tiered mineral formations at Mammoth Hot Springs in Yellowstone National Park.

Streams were slowly falling into their winter slumber. Their metabolism was slowing as they prepared for a hibernation of sorts. Like a bear in its den, the waters would disappear from view for a time but not really be gone. A warm spell may bring them back out for a short time, but for the most part, they would be holed up until spring thaw unlocked winter's grip, and they once again emerged for another season of activity. For the near term, it would be like that last hour before our own bedtime, when we feel our beings winding down and settling in. Their time for rest was near.

Looking at the thickening water during that January visit, I wondered about the fish. They would be following suit and slowing down, too. With the chilling water and reduced supply of food, the activity of all aquatic life would dwindle to only what was necessary for sustaining life. Simple existence would be the key to reaching spring thaw.

A few blustery days later, all of the once-delicate tiered formations were completely solidified and snow-covered. The fragile blossoms were gone. That day, though, held its own beauty as fine snow flittered down, sifting through the early-afternoon sun, looking like fine silver glitter riding invisible currents of air.

In October, not even a hint of that drama was visible, except for the slightly rusty color of the water. Some of the river rocks, not readily visible in January, were obviously mining rubble. One submerged rock, in fact, looked like it contained a drill hole from the old mining operation. The river was slowly doing its job of erasing the marks of man and his dreams.

In the mine site, some of the remnants of building walls were twenty feet tall or more, testifying to the human activity that once thrived. Human habitation at Nonesuch, though, was no more, except for occasional visitors like us. Nature, however, was still alive and well, slowly reclaiming the Nonesuch Mine site and town for its own.

Standing there in the crumbling shadow of what was once a sturdy industrial building, it occurred to me that when we appreciate it and work with it, nature can sustain our lives and fuel our dreams. It can also erase them and leave them in ruins when we work or fight against it.

Now as then, our task of subduing and controlling nature often turns into a life-long struggle for many people. Possibly their undoing. Yet, many continue in vain, battling to conquer nature and natural forces like they were an enemy.

I thought of how the natural world has proven to be a formidable foe indeed. Surveying the Nonesuch rubble reminded me that foes of that magnitude are better to be kept as allies.

PORKIES WILDERNESS WANDERINGS

We followed an old road, or possibly railroad grade, east out of the townsite, back down to the Little Iron. The raised grade abruptly ended at the riverbank, marking the obvious location of a long-gone bridge. The sweet scent of balsam fir drifted on the breeze as we strolled the old travel-way. A two-inch-tall fir tree stood straight in the middle of the route, ready to do its part in the reclamation.

As we explored our way back through the townsite, we noticed wild strawberry plants sprawling across portions of the meadow. Back in the day, that same area was probably mostly just bare dirt or, more likely, mud. That day in October, though, we looked around us at nature's garden, still working to heal and reclaim the land.

Venturing Out

The thermometer outside Dan's Cabin reads nine degrees Fahrenheit. Last night left a three-inch covering of fresh white on the ground, boosting the total to about eight inches. It's still blowing steady, and I think it's still snowing as well, but it's tough to tell in the dim morning light. Full daylight is still at least an hour away as we eat breakfast and pack for the day's adventure.

    Shortly after full light, we shoulder our daypacks and begin our trek up to the West Vista overlook by way of Union Spring Trail and Triple Trail. Near Crosscut Cabin, we cross what looks like a relatively fresh otter trail in the snow. Our speculation is that the otter was making its way from a small side creek over to the Union River. I'm inclined to follow the collection of footprints and slide marks to decipher more of the story, but I know we have some ground to cover in less-than-ideal conditions, so we continue on with our original plan, which eventually takes us up the back side of the ski hill. It's a steady climb through the forest that keeps us plenty warm, despite the air temperature and wintery feel of the day. Evergreens are all snow-clad, looking like winter postcard pictures. Instead of feeling bogged down by the constant climb and drooping trees, my senses are tingling, searching for whatever might be out there to find.

Once we emerge from tree cover at the top of the ski slope, we're greeted by a biting wind, plastering snow against our clothes and packs. Drifting snow prompts us to stop and put on the snowshoes that we didn't need in the sheltered forest. The resulting chill from lingering in the open motivates a little quicker pace as we navigate the top of the slopes. It's a relief when we finally get back into the cover of the forest through a small grove of hemlocks.

We emerge from the trees again at the West Vista overlook just shy of 1:00 p.m. With thick low clouds and steady snow still blowing, there isn't much vista to the vista, but we do manage to see the east end of the escarpment for a few minutes when we first arrive. The misty snow obscuring our view looks like fog settling into the range of hills surrounding Lake of the Clouds. Each rise that we can somewhat see appears a different shade of green-grey as distance increases until the backdrop is simply smoky grey. Periodically, the misty snow clears just enough to expose the most dominant trees along the nearby ridgeline before quickly swallowing them back up. At first, a few bare white patches stand out boldly near the east end of the escarpment. Then, the escarpment simply vanishes into a grey-white veil.

We are hoping to catch a few bright rays of sunshine, which were popping out now and then during our climb, but the brisk breeze, filled with crystalline flakes, cuts our stay short. So, before any brightness has a chance to return, we descend by way of the Double Trail, then backtrack out the Union Spring Trail. Snow depth is becoming more substantial by the hour, causing us to debate whether we want our snowshoes on or not. I opt to take mine off, but Julie decides to leave hers on for most of the trek out, taking them off only for the semi-well-packed local cross-country ski and snowshoe loop back to Dan's Cabin. We step in out of the snow a little more than an hour before dark, ready for a warm dinner, even though it's not really quite that time yet.

Double-checking our maps, I figure we covered at least eleven miles. Today would have been an easy day to just hunker down in the cabin, stoke the fire, and enjoy a leisurely day of reading and writing, supplemented with an occasional snack—or, maybe snacking, supplemented with some occasional reading and writing. Instead, we layered up, shouldered our daypacks, and set off into the cold and snow in search of adventure.

As always, we found adventure, even though it might not have been the adventure we set out to find. Maybe the sun didn't come out just at the right time to provide glorious photo opportunities, and we didn't capture the grand sweeping vista photographs we were hoping for, but we were still glad we ventured out into the weather, as I have been every time that I've been in a situation like this.

Today, besides the collection of new sights and experiences, the snow-laden evergreens and wintery feel of the day brought me back many years to my first winter travels here in the Porkies. Ski-touring for four days at the end of Christmas break with my friend Bill was a grand undertaking indeed. I don't remember the exact routes we took or every minute detail of the trip, but I remember the sense of pure adventure, braving the cold and embracing the thrill of bucking the risks. I remember splitting up just as dusk was turning to night, Bill heading west down the Superior shoreline, me heading east, hoping one of us would spot our intended shelter for the night, somewhere back in the trees. If not, it would be a long night in a make-shift bivouac in the snow. The shelter, the success, and the raw exhilaration were invigorating that night. I remember sliding across a downed tree with our heavy frame-packs on in order to cross a river to get to another shelter just before dark. Slipping off and landing upright in shin-deep icy water sent me to the nearby shelter to change socks and air out my ski boots before we cooked dinner in the less-than-cozy atmosphere, which was a result of the shelter having summer screening for one of its walls. Attempting to thaw a frozen water bottle near the cookstove, it got hot enough to flatten the reinforcing ribs on one side of the old milky-white soft plastic bottle. I think I still have that bottle somewhere as a reminder of that experience. From another visit, I remember sleeping in my two-person mountain tent along the Escarpment Trail in a snowstorm and waking in the morning to a collapsed tent, with frosted orange nylon laying on my face. What should have been hardships and deterrents to future excursions ended up only driving the desire for wilderness adventures even deeper.

Nearly forty years of those adventures have transpired since then, and here I am again, still venturing out into the cold and snowy wilds. I may have a little more wisdom, a touch more knowledge, and a lot more experience now, but the youthful passion for exploring and experiencing the wild hasn't changed. Safety notwithstanding, whenever I venture out, good weather or bad, I'm always glad that I did. Not that I don't sometimes have second thoughts as I'm packing up and getting ready, or wonder if I'm making the wise choice, and there have been times where "common sense" has kept me in, but I typically end up regretting when I stay indoors and avoid the discomfort of the elements. I find myself wondering what I missed and lamenting opportunities lost. On the other hand, I rarely regret going out and facing the elements, living the adventure as it comes. And, so it was today. The result wasn't exactly what we were anticipating or hoping for, but once again, the adventure certainly was.

HEMLOCKS

Stands of hemlock, large and small, dot the Porkies. With their quiet, primeval feel, they're welcome surprises all across the park. Even a small grove of hemlocks has a hushed, wild air about it.

Hemlocks are a cornerstone of the north woods. Season after season, winter, spring, summer, or fall, their color stands firm, giving no hint as to the time of year. A stand of hemlocks is a safe haven. A consistent source of shelter from the harsh glare and heat of summer or shivering cold and snow of winter. Stepping into a shadowed hemlock cathedral brings feelings of calm and safety. Sound and light are softened. Harshness fades the moment you enter. Relaxed is the mood. A hemlock grove is good company in rainstorms and snowstorms and storms of life. Their soft light is anything but dreary. It's comforting and peaceful, resonating stability and promise.

When I think of hemlocks, I often think of a late-December evening many years ago. I was a student at Michigan Tech at the time. My friend Bill and I had returned early from Christmas break to spend a few days ski-touring the Porkies backcountry, staying in one of the old screen-fronted shelters each night. They weren't much for warmth, but we didn't have to carry them in our packs like we would a tent, which left more room for other cold-weather necessities.

One particular shelter was nestled into the edge of a towering hemlock grove. My dad had passed away several months earlier, and I was still wrestling with the loss. We had spent a lot of time together in the woods, so being in the woods often brought out a parade of memories. As Bill was tending to something in the shelter, I felt drawn out into the winter woods. Even though I had never really spent much time in the company of hemlocks before, for some reason there was still a comfortably familiar feel.

As long shadows of late evening enveloped the forest, I sat down against a large hemlock, its outstretched branches spreading out like an umbrella, sheltering me from the falling snow, and listened to the quiet settling in. Sitting there in the open evening woods, somehow the cold world seemed a little warmer, and memories of my dad didn't feel so far away. I quietly sat there sorting things out for quite a while, not wanting to lose the warmth of that connection.

Eventually, a chill did begin creeping in, so I reluctantly got up and slowly worked my way back to the shelter. In time, Bill and I worked our way back out to the rest of the world and the rest of life.

I've wandered through and lingered in the hemlocks many times through the years, sometimes alone, sometimes not.

A lot of life has happened since that wintery day in the Porkies, and a lot of things have changed, with me and with the rest of the world. Groves of hemlocks, though, somehow still feel the same. Their cathedral-like timelessness seems to open doors beyond present situations and relieve burdens I often didn't even know I was carrying. Hemlock cathedrals feel like places for deep, ponderous thoughts. Places to reflect on days past or even years. The roads you've traveled and those you've traveled with feel within reach once again.

Even when I can't physically experience their tranquility, it's comforting just to know the hemlocks are out there, scattered across the north woods. Sometimes, when the rains and snows of life get heavy, I find that I still need to return to the hemlocks to pray, sort things out, and get re-synced, even if it's only in my mind.

Flowing

I needed to exit the cabin and take a walk. I don't recall the exact reason, but I believe that Julie and I weren't agreeing on something. It was probably something important, like exactly how one of us was preparing dinner, or maybe Julie was struggling with an aspect of one of her paintings, and I decided to share a comment that would have been better left unshared. Regardless, it was time for a short separation of sorts. Predictably, I ended up at the river. Something about moving water tends to soothe what needs to be soothed.

So I was standing on a bridge overlooking the Union River, watching the water flow between snow-covered banks. At first, I wasn't really focused on anything in particular or even entertaining any conscious thoughts. I was just blankly staring at the water. Then, as I became absorbed in the flow, I started thinking about how the river has been flowing, most likely, for a few thousand years. It never stops. It just keeps flowing. Through good days and bad, bounty and hardship, heat and cold, sunshine and gloom, it simply continues on. The trees along its banks were felled and carted away, exposing it to warmth and silt it had not known before. Still, it kept flowing. Ore around and maybe even beneath it was mined and carted away, exposing it to poisons it had never known and leaving buildings and relics abandoned along the river's path. Still, it kept flowing. New trees grew and died in succession, sometimes altering its flow, often changing its look. The river continued on, maybe altering its path, maybe not, depending on the interruption. Each and every year, winter snows accumulate along its banks and advance across it as ice forms and grows anywhere it can, part of the river's very being solidifying for a time. On the surface, it may appear to be halted and lifeless, yet deep down, it continues on the best that it can. If you venture close and listen, even during the deepest chill of winter, you can hear it still, its muffled voice singing its life song. Notes, pitch, and melody vary season to season, year to year, century to century, but the song remains the same. Some hear it as bright and cheery, others as solemn and melancholy, but the song is the same, the song it was created to sing.

 The river doesn't worry about other rivers or what they are doing. It doesn't concern itself with how big or small it is compared to others or how much water it carries. It doesn't fret about seasons or circumstances. It doesn't get bogged down in the politics of the day or who is in control of what. It doesn't brood about being wronged or even keep score of the incidents. It simply continues on, doing what it does.

 The river will flow and it will sing until its appointed time is done. An appropriate lesson for all of us, I thought. So often, we tend to make things more complicated and intense than they really are or need to be. We tally wrongs and rights, usually tilted in our favor. We fret and fume about things that haven't even happened and quite likely won't ever come to pass. We spend much too much of our time absorbed in unimportant things or fixated on trivial matters that will soon fade away.

   Standing there on the bridge in the softening evening light, with the river flowing through my head, it was all so clear and easy to understand. I wiped the slate clean, turned my attention to things that mattered, and slowly strolled back to the cabin.

Nonesuch Trout

A welcoming party of mosquitoes greeted me at the trailhead as I was packing up my gear. On a day in late May where temperatures were predicted to get into the eighties, I would normally opt to wade wet. But, as I was liberally dowsing myself with bug spray, I decided that some extra protection would be a good idea, so I pulled on my waders in between swats. The belt that I always wear to keep most of the river on the outside, should I lose my footing, doubled as a good bug barrier to keep the biters on the outside, too.

It was only about 8:00 a.m., but the thermometer was rising fast. I expected the hike to the river would be hot and buggy but was pleasantly surprised to find that I was wrong. There was just enough shade to moderate the heat, and the bugs apparently decided to wait at the trailhead for the next potential meal instead of following me. I had no idea why—they usually just swarm the first candidate and keep at it—but I considered it one of those blessings that I don't understand and just said, "thank you."

With my mind set on fishing, I only gave the Nonesuch mine site ruins a few passing glances on my way through to the river. Like most ghost towns, it seemed to have a lonely air about it, like it was waiting for its wayward souls to return.

When I emerged from the riverside trees, I was surprised by how shallow the river was. With the calendar page still on May, I expected the flow to be much more substantial. I guess it shouldn't have been such a surprise because we had experienced moderate snow during the winter and a relatively slow spring melt that started early. Spring rains had been frugal as well, leaving most of the streams near home—which was only a few hours away—looking like late August. The Little Iron proved to be no different.

The plunge pool at the base of Nonesuch Falls looked like my best fishing prospect, so after looking it over for a few minutes, I rigged up my fly rod and began plying its depths with a bead-headed nymph. After fifteen minutes of wetting the nymph, I switched over to a yellow stimulator because I refused to believe that there wasn't a trout in the pool. First, I tried dropping the fly directly into the falls and letting it tumble into the pool. Then, I tried dropping it here, there, and anywhere I hadn't yet tried.

Although water cascaded into the pool across most of the width of the river, there was more of a concentrated flow coming into the south side, so I focused more of my attention on that area. Overall, though, I pretty well covered the entire pool from a variety of casting locations.

After another fifteen minutes or so of imagining each cast was going to be the one, I still wasn't convinced that the pool held nothing but water. My intention for the day, though, wasn't strictly fishing. I wanted to explore a decent stretch of the Little Iron just for the sake of seeing the sights and getting to know the river. With that in mind, I bid the pool—and probably a few fish—goodbye and began slowly working my way upstream, tossing a fly any place that looked like it might hold a fish.

The entire river bottom was solid bedrock strewn with small collections of fragments and slabs. Woody cover was sparse. In fact, calling it sparse is being generous. Still, it was a beautiful little river with its interesting bottom contours and formations, riffles and runs, cascades, chutes, and bends. Due to low water levels, though, most of the holes were not really holes. They were more like smooth depressions, extending the water depth to twelve inches instead of six. Even with the reddish iron tint of the water, bottom features were clearly visible most everywhere. Fish were not.

I continued my upstream exploration for roughly three hours without hooking—or even seeing—a fish. Well, that's not quite true. I did see a few minnows, but instead of seeing a few minnows at a time, as is usually the case, I only saw a few minnows. Period.

Besides the lack of cover, I later suspected that the water temperature may have been getting a little too warm as well. Especially for that early in the year. Unfortunately, the idea of getting out my thermometer and checking didn't occur to me until later in the evening when I was reflecting on the day's events while gazing into a campfire. So I couldn't really say if the water temperature was an issue or not. You would think that I would have thought of something important like that while I was still on the river, but, being so early in the season, water temperatures getting too high isn't a typical issue, so it just didn't click.

As the heat and bugs both continued to increase, I decided to turn around and do some exploring below the falls. It took about an hour to retrace my steps back to Nonesuch Falls. At that point, I considered fishing the falls pool again but decided to explore some more new water instead. I was torn between focusing on the best potential fish-holding water at hand and simply exploring a new area of the park. With heat and bugs beginning to make fishing difficult, I opted to continue downstream to see the sights, test some new water, and see if I could find another good-looking fishing spot.

Just like above the falls, there wasn't much in the way of cover in the water. I found a lot of beautiful flowing water over interesting sculpted rock, but no fish. I explored down to where the old road or railroad grade crossed the river, then a little beyond that. At that point, I was beginning to find some woody cover in the river. In fact, there was a sizeable logjam where I made my final casts. As I was closely watching my fly, taking great care not to do anything to disturb its natural drift, I was also watching mosquitoes lining up along the knuckles of my rod hand. Anything I did to shoo them away also resulted in unnatural behavior of my fly. As I contemplated a remedy, beads of sweat were beginning to ooze out from under my hatband and trickle down my forehead.

At that point, I decided that the best remedy would be to move my explorations to somewhere with at least a mild breeze to keep bugs and heat at bay. So, at least on that particular day, the trout around Nonesuch Falls turned out to be nonesuch as well.

My roughly three-quarter-mile wader-clad stroll back out to the trailhead was relatively bug-free. As long as I was moving, biting bugs seemed to be absent. I assumed that maybe the heat had them feeling a bit lethargic, so they didn't bother to chase me. Normally the mid-eighty-degree heat would have me feeling lethargic, too, but it somehow didn't seem to bother me much. Maybe I was just so appreciative of the lack of blackflies and mosquitoes that other distractions went unnoticed.

I tried imagining what it would have been like back in the days when the town and mine were bustling with activity. With no window screens, head-nets, or bug spray, I'm not sure how well I would have handled the living conditions. Even with those protections, bug season here in the UP can be trying—which was why I was heading back to the trailhead. It gave me an appreciation for the fortitude of those pioneering people.

As for the fishing, I had experienced some similar rivers in the Upper Peninsula before. High on visual aesthetics. Low on fish. Persistence usually pays off in those cases. In this case, the heat and bugs had simply out-persisted my persistence. Still, I found that even a day of fishing that ended up just being a day of exploring new water while wetting some flies was a worthwhile endeavor, as it usually is. Fortunately, I wasn't counting on having fish for dinner. I hoped that Julie wasn't counting on it either.

Bugs

I hate bugs. Well, not all bugs. In fact, not most bugs. Just mosquitoes, and biting flies of all sizes, shapes, and colors. The rest of the bugs are fine—as long as they're not in my house, that is. Or my vehicle.

It's not actually the bugs that I hate (we're back to the fly and mosquito discussion); it's what they do. I hate being bitten because I get a considerable welt from the bites, and the bump lasts quite a while in some cases. I especially hate getting bit on the head and neck. For one thing, bites on the head and neck seem to itch worse than other bites. Or, maybe the itch is just more noticeable in those areas. Anyway, the other issue is that head and neck bites are so visible, and they look pretty bad.

Of course, it seems like at least half of the bites I get *are* on my head or neck. Biting bugs seem naturally attracted to the head. Maybe it's because, on most animals, that's the main area where vulnerable skin exists, so bugs go where they have the most access to bitable skin. Or, maybe it's because more heat is expelled from an animal's head. That's especially true for people. The other possible explanation is that biting insects are just plain evil, so they go for the most annoying bite location possible—the head.

Personally, I tend to lean toward thinking that biting bugs are just plain evil. That makes me feel better about hating them. It also makes giving them a good smashing slap more gratifying. Now I understand the ecological side of it. How bugs of all kinds fit perfectly into the grand web of life. That they are an important link in the food chain, and how they provide other benefits to the overall environmental system. I get all that, but personally, I still hate 'em. There have been times where I know that I've heard their buzzing change to a sinister laugh. I'm sure others have heard it, too, but are afraid to admit it for fear of someone questioning their mental health. I have no worries there. My mental health is often in question anyway.

Besides the sinister buzzing laughter, biting bugs hunt in packs and work in cooperation to overcome their victim's defenses. I consider that to be premeditated, and I think it's provable in court. Countless times I have had a decoy insect buzzing around my face, keeping my attention, while an accomplice—or accomplices—sneaks in for a quick neck or back-of-the-head shot.

The most aggravating thing about it is how often I fall for it. You would think that after more than fifty years, I would be wise to their little distraction ploy, but so crafty are those little beasts that they pull me into their diabolical scheme time after time.

Did I mention their hunting in packs? Actually, gangs would be a more appropriate term. They prowl in gangs, looking for innocent victims to maul. And I get mauled frequently. Sometimes it's in a dark alley-like trail, but sometimes it's right in the open, in broad daylight. They have no shame!

PORKIES WILDERNESS WANDERINGS

I recall a time when I was in the Union Bay Campground, enjoying the bugless freedom of a cool stiff breeze coming in off of Superior, basking in the late-May sunshine. Then, the breeze faltered. The lull couldn't have lasted more than twenty seconds, but in the midst of the calm, they launched their attack. At first, it was blackflies leading the assault. Later, though, as a few clouds moderated the sun's intensity, mosquitoes joined into the festivities during slight pauses in the breeze. Even though there were witnesses around, the vicious beasts openly assailed me with reckless abandon.

Another time, I had been fishing the Little Iron River, then stopped by the Union River for a few casts—okay, quite a few casts—before returning to camp. I knew that I had suffered a few bug-bites on my back, but I was marveling at how those insidious fiends know the precise area between your shoulder blades that is completely unreachable by either hand. They casually dine while you madly flail the air and harmlessly slap nearby. To make the predicament even worse, neither hand can reach the itch either, leaving you to writhe around in your camp chair like you've got a personal problem of some sort. Or, like a bear, you have to resort to rubbing against a nearby tree—as a side note, never use an evergreen tree because they tend to get your shirt all sappy.

Anyway, you get the point. I hate bugs. Well, not all bugs...

Union River Fishing

Standing on the wooden footbridge, watching the Little Union trickle past, "skinny" was the best description that I could think of. It wasn't much for width or depth, and it certainly wasn't what I would call trout water. Then again, I couldn't help thinking about the little unnamed creek near home, where I helped a couple of NMU graduate students do some electro-shocking as part of their research projects. Even though my four-year-old granddaughter could've readily hopped across it in most locations without a splash, I remembered taking measurements on a twelve-inch brook trout we netted out of there, not to mention the sixteen-inch salmon. Still, on the Little Union, I was concerned about stressing the fish too much in such small water during the August heat, so I decided to retrace my steps back down the trail to the Union River.

The Union wasn't carrying what I would call an abundance of water, but it at least looked more like a river than a minnow creek. Just as I was approaching the old steel bridge, a family came out of the trail along the other side of the river with two young boys carrying fishing poles and a plastic container of worms. The dad told me not to worry. The boys had only caught one small trout.

I wasn't exactly concerned about the one small one the boys had caught. It was all the others that were probably now hiding hither and yon. My aspirations shriveled like one of the boy's worms caught out on open pavement during an afternoon heat wave. But I had been wanting to fish that stretch of water since first seeing it back in January when I was trying to decipher the river through its armor of ice and snow. So I proceeded with my short hike down the trail from which the family had just emerged. When I was a hundred yards or so past the confluence with the Little Union, I strung up my fly rod, tied on a yellow stimulator fly, and stepped in.

With warm weather and relatively shallow water, I wasn't wearing waders, just old hiking shoes. The water felt colder than I expected as it seeped in, which was good from a trout standpoint. I stood for a few minutes in the coolness. My purpose for pausing there in the water for a bit was to scrutinize river details and determine where to best place my first cast. What I found myself doing, though, was simply taking in the flowing scenery. Small stair-stepping falls, cascades, fast chutes, riffles, runs, and pools. I could see every detail of the river bottom in all but the deepest pools, which meant that trout would be able to readily see me, too. Even though I was dressed in drab, earthy tones, I still wasn't as camouflaged as a trout. The advantage, as usual, was theirs.

I slowly began probing each potential fish-holding feature with my imitation meal. In the relatively shallow, clear flow, most features were visibly barren of fish, but from experience, I knew better than to simply trust my vision. Wild creatures are colored and patterned the way they are for a reason. So I continued probing each feature as I slowly ventured upstream. For the most part, I wouldn't say that I was actually casting. Due to close quarters and well-placed vegetation, more often than not what guided my fly was more of a flick or a wave of the rod tip. Whatever was needed to place the fly where it needed to be, or in some cases, close to where it needed to be.

One particular spot was not visibly barren of fish. The trout in question looked to be a rainbow of about ten inches. It was tucked under the curvature of an enormous boulder in a location that was plainly visible yet maddeningly difficult to get a fly into. Several attempts from a number of locations failed to put my fly within a foot of the calmly finning fish. The spot that I envisioned I needed to be was easily visible to the fish and already occupied by a sprawling tree branch. I stepped back and watched from a distance, trying to develop a plan. The plan I finally settled on was to quietly continue my tour upstream.

That's where I found an old stone and cement foundation section that looked like a short wall extending across the river. Near the middle, there was a broken-out section a few feet wide, creating a fast chute that emptied into a dark hole in the sandstone riverbed. That dark pool drew my attention.

Several times my fly swirled through the pool, sometimes visible, sometimes not. With each pass, my hope faded. Then came the flashing of a fish and the pulsing of my line. The small rainbow thrashed its way up from the darkness and into my net. I could have readily landed the fish without the aid of a net, but I always try to minimize the stress on the fish, even the small ones. It wasn't the colorfully painted brook trout that I was hoping for, but it was a trout, and a wild one at that. A steelhead smolt, most likely, waiting for the proper time in its lifecycle to move out to the Big Lake, where it would grow and mature until it was ready to return to the river to start another generation of fish. As I turned the shiny-sided trout loose from the confines of my net, it bolted back to its secret hideout in the darkness without a moment of hesitation.

I lingered for a time, thinking about that fish and how dependent it was, not only on the river but the entire Union River watershed. Actually, the entire Lake Superior watershed would affect that fish during the course of its life, much like all of us who live, or even recreate, here near the Big Lake.

Those thoughts continued to swirl through my head as I slowly worked my way up the river, past the old iron bridge, and on up through the slight canyon, to where the Union passes beneath South Boundary Road.

I saw a few other small trout, but none came to my net. One did rise up from the safety of a rock undercut fortress to dance with my fly for a moment as it spun in the swirling current. The fish, caught up in the same swirl, stared at my fly, working on its decision, as they both slowly rotated in a clockwise circle. The fish ultimately decided that something wasn't right and casually descended back down to the safety of its hiding place beneath the undercut.

Fishing up through the canyon proved to be difficult. Not because of difficult flow characteristics or slipperiness of the rocks, which were indeed minor factors, but because of scenic distractions. Stair-step cascades over moss-covered rock, lichen-accented walls rising up into the forest from the river, and shade-producing trees contributing an air of lushness. Being there was a success, regardless of fish in the net or not. Fishing became intermingled with sightseeing, or maybe sightseeing became intermingled with fishing. It was difficult to tell which was the dominant activity. I tried to imagine my surroundings in the fireworks display of October. Knowing my imagination couldn't even hope to live up to that reality, I decided to simply wait and see. I'd be back for the celebration.

The twin convoluted steel culverts—both easily ten feet in diameter—carrying the Union flow under South Boundary Road marked the end of my outing, not because of lack of fish or fishable water beyond, but because my time for the day's adventure was winding down. A collection of logs and sticks against the upstream end of the culverts throttled down the flow, leaving water in the structures only a few inches deep. Looking up through one of the tunnels, the kid in me just couldn't resist, so I carefully waded on through and climbed out over the barricade of wooden debris.

I considered continuing on for a bit, regardless of the time. Then I realized that I had already accomplished what I had set out to do. I had fished the river that I so often envisioned fishing during our January stay—dancing with trout, and even admiring one in my hand. I had stepped into the refreshing flow, felt its pulse, and been part of its existence. After spending some time rejuvenating in our natural world, I was leaving it unscathed for anyone that would come after me. Continuing on would have been fun, I'm sure, but it was time to go. Time to have a bite to eat and to reflect in the flicker of a campfire flame. It was time to go sit beside the expanse of Superior, look out to the fading horizon, and begin dreaming of tomorrow.

LITTLE CARP TROUT

The sun had finally emerged after a few days of overcast and wet. With it came the warmth and mugginess of August. Fortunately, I'd be spending a good share of the day standing in cold running water.

Sunlight mingled with a misty haze through the hemlocks as my wife and I stood on the bridge near Overlooked Falls, surveying the Little Carp River. I had been there a couple of days prior, doing a little river reconnaissance, wishing I was fishing. This time I had fly fishing gear in my daypack, ready for some actual exploration. I was there to be an active participant instead of just an intense spectator.

The air felt heavy with moisture. Not quite to the point of a sauna, but more like a closed-up bathroom after a hot shower. I could see it in the hazy shafts of light that penetrated the shadowed forest. Just looking at the river felt like a refreshing drink. I was tempted to rig up my fly rod and step into the sparkling flow right there at the bridge, but I didn't really know the river, so I knew it would be more fruitful to do a little more exploring and watching from the trail first. Even without the heat and humidity, my first temptation is always to just step right in as soon as I arrive at a river before I even attempt to look things over and size up the situation. Besides, I wanted to fish my way up the river, not down. So I held back my temptation to plunge in, and we headed off down the trail to see what promising-looking water we could find, my wife looking for painting inspiration and me looking for a good place to catch trout.

Our pace was quicker than normal for studying the water because I wanted to cover some ground before I committed to fishing for fear that there might be a better-looking spot just a little farther downstream. I was also getting a bit distracted by the landscape, so I wasn't paying as much careful attention to the water as I should have. I often find myself studying vegetation and topography, trying to surmise what once was and how it got to be as it is—basically strolling along the trail and thinking.

As we passed the cabin near Greenstone Falls, I found myself feeling a little envious of the family that was staying there. Besides having a gorgeous view, they were perched right in the middle of an enticing stretch of trout water, with the sounds of the river permeating the forest. I made a mental note that someday we'd have to experience staying there. Until then, I would have to accept the fact that it was someone else's adventure to live. At the present time, I was living a different adventure.

A little north of Greenstone Falls Cabin, the trail climbed a ridge to skirt around a small camp area. Up on the ridge, the river was far enough away that details were not really discernible. We could see the river, but not well enough to evaluate fishing possibilities. After what seemed like at least half a mile, the trail finally dropped back down from the ridge and onto a flat floodplain. We took the opportunity to wander back over near the river. That's where we found a boulder that was roughly seven feet tall and ten feet across, perched in the woods. There was a sixteen-inch diameter yellow birch and an eleven-inch diameter hemlock growing atop the boulder, with their roots extending down the sides of the rock to reach nourishing soil. There was also the skeleton of what was once a six-inch diameter cedar clinging to the top of the boulder.

Based on the size of surrounding hemlocks, ground level hadn't changed much in the immediate area in quite some time. So I could only surmise that the boulder had once been encapsulated in a mound of soil, and after the trees became established atop the mound, the soil eroded away to leave the trees stranded on the boulder. They had substantial roots extending down to the ground and appeared to be in good condition, so I assumed they would survive for quite a while before joining the cedar in its state of decomposition.

I was tempted to continue following the river, but I did want to actually fish, not just survey the possibilities. I probably should've just rigged up there and started fishing, but I really liked the looks of the water from the camp area on up to the bridge near Overlooked Falls. That stretch was likely fished pretty heavily and had more foot traffic right along the river bank, but I still decided that was where I wanted to fish, so we headed back upstream along the trail. By then, I wasn't really taking in the scenery as much as just covering ground so that I could start fishing.

Standing on the bedrock formations a short way below Greenstone Falls, I found it difficult to get my fly rod rigged up because I kept staring at the river instead of my gear. When I finally stepped into the flow, the chill of the water was like opening a refrigerator on a hot, sultry day. As with the previous day's fishing, I was wading wet to avoid having to haul my waders around. Most of the water was relatively shallow anyway, making full waders a hot, cumbersome overkill. Hip-boots would have worked fine, but they still would have been much heavier and bulkier than the extra pair of hiking shoes I was carrying in my daypack. Besides, I didn't own hip-boots, so it didn't matter anyway. So I was wading wet, which is a refreshing way to go in August when you're fishing relatively shallow streams with a good solid bottom. As Julie started setting up to do some painting, I pointed my wet shoes upstream and began fishing.

Just below Greenstone Falls, I was floating a yellow stimulator over a small hole that was guarded by a sizeable boulder. I watched a nine-inch brook trout rise up from the shadows and quickly snatch my fly. The frenzied pulsing at the end of my line was as refreshing as the flow. After taking the fish from my net and briefly admiring its wild flare, I opened my hand and watched it dart back to the unknown.

Not far above the falls, I was fishing my way through a swift run when I was surprised to catch a glimpse of a trout that looked to be about twelve inches long shoot out in front of me and race downstream. It had been holding near a log in the shallows by the riverbank. My attention had been focused on the run that was closer to the middle of the river. Before I spooked the fish, I did take a look around, but I blew off the shallow water near the bank in favor of the run, which I thought was a much better bet. As it turned out, I lost the bet.

I saw a few other trout that afternoon, but none came to my net. I did get the satisfaction, though, of fishing water I had been wanting to fish for several months. I had finally lived the adventure I had been picturing in my mind, just without as many fish. Due to easy access and proximity to a couple of popular waterfalls, I knew the stretch I had chosen to fish was probably well-used, not only by people fishing but by general sightseers as well. It could also have been the mostly-sunny, muggy day, or maybe my choice of fly patterns. My presentation of the fly may not have been at its best either. It's usually easy to come up with a list of reasons for a day short on fish. Still, exploring with my fly rod, I had the privilege of being an active participant in the life of the river. Even though I was traveling in the opposite direction as the river, I was flowing over the rocks just the same.

Not long before I reached the bridge where I had planned to end my explorations, I came across a young boy that I guessed was probably about seven or eight years old. He was playing in the middle of the river, moving rocks and splashing around as kids often do, while a lady that I presumed was his mother lounged on the far bank and watched.

I was a bit bummed that I had to get out of the water in order to politely go around him without intruding on his space. I wasn't upset, or even irritated, really, just a little bothered about the interruption. Still, I was pleasant about it, smiling at the boy and nodding to the mother. After all, they weren't doing anything wrong.

As I was stepping back into the flow, just upstream, it occurred to me that when I was his age, I would no doubt have been playing in the water, too. Then the thought hit me that I *am* playing in the water. In fact, I've been playing in the water most of my life. It may not keep me physically young, but I do believe it's at least part of what keeps me young at heart and always planning new adventures.

I looked back at the boy again and gave him a nod of approval. He didn't see me, but I felt I needed to do it anyway. Hopefully, he'll never lose that youthful urge to play in the water.

There wasn't much river left to fish before my planned exit point. It was mostly just the plunge pools below a couple of small falls. With the pools being much deeper than anywhere else I had fished that day, I'm sure I didn't have enough weights on the line to get my fly down to where it needed to be to actually entice a fish. At that point, it didn't really matter anyway. Sometimes, just the act of fishing and the anticipation that comes with it are all it takes to satisfy our need for adventure. For me, just stepping into the flow often provides the connection I need.

Later, as I stood dripping on the bridge above the falls, my young friend walked by with his parents. I wanted to say something to them, but in the spur of the moment, I couldn't think of anything that I thought would sound appropriate. So, I simply smiled and nodded. Based on the way the dad nodded back, I was pretty sure that he knew what I meant.

Union River Visions

We had just arrived at Dan's Cabin for our October artist-in-residence, but we decided to forgo getting settled in. Instead, we quickly gulped down some mid-afternoon lunch snacks and headed out to reacquaint ourselves with the neighborhood.

First, we ventured up the trail to the Little Union River crossing. Water was still skimpy, just like it was when we visited in August. Maple and yellow birch leaves collected on the rocks, stream bank, gravel bars, and in slow water. Submerged leaves lit up the bottom of a small plunge pool where the river gurgled down a miniature chute between two boulders. A yellow-orange maple leaf floated like a toy boat through the pool to join up with a mass of sodden amber leaves blocking the next chute, apparently held back by a stick lodged in the rocks. Everywhere were orange and amber leaves, in the trees and on the ground. The woods were possessed with an amber glow.

We moved over to the Union River, where there was more water to explore. It, too, looked much like it did when I fished it during our August visit. The large pool that always captivated me by the hill in the trail was full of yellow, floating freely, swirling with the current, and hovering at the bottom as a mirror image of what was above. It looked like a fishing hole, but I didn't see any fish. Of course, that was likely because they saw me first.

Looking at my surroundings, standing there by the water, I came to realize that we would be taking a monumental number of pictures during our roughly two-week stay. With autumn in full swing, there was just too much to take in and retain. I would need lots of memory-jogging pictures. As Julie gave the shutter a workout, I continued upstream through the flow of colors.

About a hundred yards above the bridge near the Union River Outpost Campground, there is a deep hole created by a ledge that crosses the river. It's round and sculpted, somewhat dark near the bottom. I had fished it expectantly in August, to no avail. As I stood peering into the sculpted bowl, with gently swirling water holding a collection of yellow leaves captive at the bottom, I noticed a rhythmic movement. This wasn't a swirling leaf. This was purposeful motion. Slowly, a light-toned trout eased backward out of the tannin darkness, paralleled by a much darker trout, both probably eight inches in length. They were side-by-side, following the same rhythm. They slowly swirled in unison, then set out on a slow cruise of the hole. As they turned, I noticed the telltale white-trimmed lower fins of a brook trout. While they made their way upstream through the bowl, I lost sight of them in an area bright with glare. With a tall, thin cascade feeding the hole, I knew they hadn't continued moving upstream. They were still there in the hole. Somewhere.

After a few minutes of searching, my eyes carefully scanning back and forth, investigating every detail, I saw them sliding back downstream along the same basic route they had followed on their way upstream. They didn't linger long in front of me before they cautiously rose toward the surface and slipped out of the pool and into shallow water, crossing the sandstone river bottom atop the ledge. As they crossed the shallows down to a much smaller hole, their markings, enhanced by the approach of spawning season, stood out as boldly as a magazine picture. Drifting over blushed sandstone, it looked like they were in the palm of a great outstretched hand, holding them out for me to see. The only time I've ever seen brook trout details that clearly was after a successful fly rod cast when I was holding one of those miracles in the palm of my own hand, admiring its intricate artwork.

It was after the pair again disappeared into an area bright with glare that I lost track of them. That's when I got caught up in the downstream view of a series of cascades and pools through red sandstone and amber leaves—maple, aspen, and yellow birch, with an occasional red maple leaf adding flair. Even a few of the aspen leaves sported bright red colorings in the collections entrapped in rocks, gravel, and shallows. By that time, Julie had rejoined me from where ever it was that she had been taking pictures. After climbing a little farther upstream, exploring that series of cascades, we decided to retrace our steps back to the cabin to prepare for an evening visit to Lake of the Clouds. I wasn't exactly done exploring the river, but I left with the comforting realization that there *would* be more river explorations in the coming days.

In fact, there would be more explorations all over the park. We had the luxury of time and freedom to roam. With more than two weeks of unscheduled time ahead of us, I felt like a schoolkid going into summer vacation. The world was a wide-open playground.

SEASONS

I could hear heavy rain on the roof and strong gusts of wind howling through the early morning darkness. Daylight dawned to reveal the sullen sky that was still producing on-and-off showers—nothing threatening or foreboding, just blah. In fact, the sky wasn't even what I would call dismal. I was surprised every time it rained because I thought sure the rains were done. As I was thinking that, a loud rumble of thunder resonated through the cabin. So I ended up sitting out on the covered porch, sipping maple-ginger tea, trying to decide on a plan for the day.

Well, we had actually already decided on a plan—hike the Summit Peak loop and then tour the Presque Isle Falls area—but the viability of that plan had come into question. We were still hoping the sky would get tired of raining sometime in the morning, allowing us time for implementing a slightly condensed or maybe just a little less relaxed plan by afternoon.

As I thought about it, it occurred to me that my current predicament seemed to be the theme for fall: anxiously waiting for the weather or other obligations to clear so we could get out and experience the glory of autumn.

In winter, the landscape doesn't change much. Sure, snow depth changes, and powdery snow gives things a different look and feel than wet, clingy snow, but the landscape usually bounces back and forth between the two basic looks multiple times during the season. Rivers and streams do freeze up to a different look, but they often thaw out again prior to the formal spring break-up. In general, you don't lose the look and feel of winter throughout most of the season.

Spring certainly has its progression of changes. There's a parade of flowers as trees and shrubs slowly green up. Biting insects emerge, but that's not big news, just something to lament. Most people, including me, seem to welcome the progression of spring, feeling more relaxed as the changes occur.

Summer, well, with its heat, humidity, and progression of biting insects, just seems to linger. There is a changing of the guard in the flower world, and we look forward to the growth of various fruits and vegetables. To me, though, summer is basically just something I have to endure and get through. I only lamented its passing when I was in school, and the end of summer meant the beginning of the freedom-ending classroom.

Fall is different. Fall produces a sense of urgency. Things often start out mellow enough. Usually by mid-August, a few impatient leaves begin their transition. It's subtle at first. Biting bugs, particularly mosquitoes, are seriously waning, and we get those occasional days of mild temperatures and low humidity. Those are the things, along with the realization that trout season is sliding toward its end and hunting season is nearing reality, that awaken me from my summer-induced coma. In late August, I begin to come alive again. Soon, mugginess will be virtually forgotten, and the high temperatures of the day will be comfortable and relaxing instead of oppressive and foreboding. Life begins to feel good again.

Optimism is on the rise—at least for me it is. Winter is far enough in the future that it doesn't yet pose a threat, and summer is beginning to show in the rearview mirror. My time of year is at hand.

The first red or yellow leaf that I see on the ground usually catches me by surprise. I always think that it's way too early. Then I begin looking around more closely and realize that lone, bright leaf on the ground is not really a loner. It's part of a movement. Color is catching on. It usually starts out in the swamps and bogs. More often than not, maples are the front-runners. Those bright crimson patches dotting wet areas soon spread. Before long, it's not just wet areas. Random branches throughout the forest are set ablaze. Birches, especially yellow birches, join in. Then in mid-September, I begin noticing that even "green" leaves are no longer the deep, rich greens of summer. Yellowish-green becomes a better description. It becomes more noticeable each day. This is when I usually start wanting to apply the brakes to the wheels of autumn. Somehow, though, the more I try to apply the brakes, the more the season seems to accelerate. That's when a sense of panic begins to set in, as I realize that autumn is once again passing its prime. The downward slide into winter is not far off. Soon, there will be more color on the ground than on the branches. That, to me, is truly peak color time. When the entire forest glows with an amber glow. Reds and oranges do their part, too, but it's the shades of yellow that generate the warmth of autumn's glow. Warmth is short-lived, though, sometimes lasting only a handful of days. Then a coolness creeps in as branches become bare and warm colors cure to rust and brown, carpeting forest floors. Darkness is intruding farther into each day. Somewhere in the mix of this transition comes the mingling of snow crystals. At first, just for brief visits. The duration of those visits begins to grow until one day we realize that white is the new normal. That cold blanket is here for a long stay. Warmth is past.

For the moment, though, I was trying hard to hold back the flow of autumn. To hold on to the warmth. Looking forward to basking in the warm glow and cool air. Trying to savor autumn once more, because color season is fleeting at best. I feel like I'm constantly rushing around, trying to soak in all of the brilliance of the season before it's gone. I find myself wanting to be everywhere, every day, so as not to miss any of nature's autumn glory. Rain and wind feel like thieves, robbing me of autumn's beauty. Every day not spent reveling in fall colors feels like a day lost that I will never get back. At times, I even get to the point of fretting about it, lamenting the loss.

So there I sat, on the cabin porch, laying plans, not wanting the opportunities of a fleeting autumn day to pass me by.

As noon approached, rains became stronger again, with the feeling that it had settled in for a much longer stay than I had hoped. The breeze had picked up again as well, carrying a faint mist into the covered porch that I could feel tickling my face. Leaves weren't coming down quite as plentiful as raindrops, but during gusts, it was a close race. Color season was quickly winding down. It appeared that there was beginning to be more color on the ground than on the branches. My sense of urgency was rising. We arrived at the Porkies knowing that colors would be disappearing while we were there. I was just hoping it would be later rather than sooner. Autumn winds were my enemy, or at least it felt that way.

I thought a little about time, how hours and days sometimes seem to straggle. Weeks and months somehow maintain a much quicker pace. Seasons seem to disappear almost before they arrive. Years go by almost as fast as vacations. Our lives are governed by time, but time certainly isn't governed, or even affected, by our lives.

As time ticked away, the falling of leaves seemed to be constant. I feared that the shower of leaves would cease only when there were no more leaves to fall. Some oaks and beeches would hold on to some of their leaves until spring buds forced the issue, but other trees were giving up their leaves with reckless abandon. They would soon be left shamelessly bare to face the chills of winter.

Each gust of wind became painful for me to hear. I was almost afraid to look out at the downpour of leaves being dashed to the ground. It felt like if I didn't look or acknowledge it was happening, somehow it wouldn't. But I couldn't help looking. Like when a close friend or loved one is going away for a long time, you don't want to see them go, but you don't want to miss the sight of them leaving either. Watching them leave seems to extend the time that they're there. So I continued to watch.

About 3:00 p.m., the rains and wind let up. Within minutes, clouds broke up and the sun emerged. We decided it was getting too late in the day to make the nearly thirty-mile trek over to Presque Isle Falls. Instead, we decided to just quietly amble around the cabin area. Even though we had explored that area before, there's always more to see and experience.

The ground was every bit as colorful as the trees. Things had certainly changed within the past couple of days. Autumn was moving quickly.

First, we simply followed a small dry creek bed down to the Little Union River, probably only a hundred yards downstream from our cabin. We found a series of cascading falls running in ribbons over mossy bedrock, meandering through a gathering of rust and amber leaves. Tranquility in motion. Our little Canon point-and-shoot camera just couldn't capture what my emotions felt. Try as I might— different locations, different angles, different settings—the pixels just didn't match my mind's eye vision of what I was immersed in. Softness. Contrast of colors and textures. Singing water. Interplay of sunlight and shadow. The daily drama of existence in the north woods of the Porkies.

I couldn't find any trout in the pools below the cascading falls, but I knew that was a temporary condition. At certain times of the year, or maybe even certain times of day, they would be there. I wanted to be there then, too, to fish those inviting pools. I wanted to actively participate in the fluid drama unfolding there in the peacefulness of the hemlocks. Other trees were edging into the streamside hemlock forest as well—a blend of sugar maples and yellow birch—but hemlocks were the primary inhabitants, witnesses of the drama of flowing water through a north woods forest. It was peaceful and quiet but far from silent. I closed my eyes for a moment, like the shutter of a camera after exposing a scene, trying to capture the experience in my mind.

At that point, Julie lingered in the vicinity of the cabin, working on ideas for her next painting. Her intent was to eventually follow the trail over to the Union River, where we would reunite. I continued following the Little Union down its winding, rocky channel, like a droplet of water joining the flow. I shared its journey, savored its sensations with all my senses, and imagined its variations through the seasons. Trying to take it all in was verging on sensory overload. I tried the camera again. Still, it wasn't up to the task.

Only a talented artist could possibly come close to capturing the essence of that masterpiece of God.

My intent was to follow the Little Union down to its confluence with the Union River, then follow the Union up to the hole where I'd watched a couple of brook trout a few days prior. Somehow, I expected it wouldn't take long to make the trek because it didn't seem like it would be all that far, although I had never actually followed that entire route before.

I was surprised to find the stream distance was considerably farther than trail distance, even though I knew that was usually the case. The rough map in my head just didn't picture enough land in that area to allow for so much meandering of the stream. I reached my destination, expecting my wife, Julie, to already be there waiting for me and wondering what took me so long. As it turned out, she had gotten sidetracked poking around near the cabin with her Nikon SLR camera, which, in hindsight, I should have expected. That day was our 35th wedding anniversary, so you would think that we would have been able to do a better job of predicting what each other was up to. We obviously still had work to do in that area.

Even though sunlight was gone from the river gorge, autumn's radiance certainly was not. Glowing leaf art still highlighted the ribbons of water cascading over moss-covered rock. Walking the forest trail back toward our cabin, I was amazed at how brilliant the ground was as a result of the day of wind and rain. Newscasters had been advertising autumn as being well past its peak, but looking around, it looked to be in its prime to me.

We wrapped up our anniversary day with a dinner of venison steaks cooked over a wood fire, fried sweet potatoes, and diced peaches. It may not sound like a big deal to most people, but in a cozy cabin nestled into the north woods, it tasted like a feast. After dinner, we spent the last couple hours of our day with me writing and Julie painting watercolor sketches by candlelight and headlamp. That may sound a lot like work, but to us, it was just a natural extension of spending a wilderness day steeped in autumn, trying to extend the enchantment of the season.

RAINED OUT PLANS

Individual clouds weren't discernible. In fact, the entire sky just looked like a dark, lumpy sponge ready to be squeezed out. Our intent for the day was to hike the roughly fifteen-mile Government Peak loop, starting at the Cuyahoga Creek trailhead. The day didn't look promising, but a plan was a plan.

After changing my mind about the direction of travel a couple of times, I decided that we should do the escarpment section first. My thought was that by going that way first, we would at least see the panoramic views from the escarpment with some remaining autumn color, even if our trek got cut short by rain. That thought may very well have sealed our fate.

We headed up the rocky trail with a slight drizzle already underway. I was surprised how yellow the woods still were, but then I remembered the swath of color near Superior that we had seen the day before from our vantage point on Summit Peak. Inside the swath, the damp woods radiated autumn's farewell. I soon noticed that the vast majority of the color was on the Superior side of the escarpment. To the south were mostly bare trunks and branches, except for a smattering of rusty oaks and an occasional aspen still showing off.

Passing the Cuyahoga Mine site, I stopped to read a ragged old Department of Natural Resources sign that was warning people not to disturb anything around the mine. Looking around at what simply looked like a mound in the woods with a trench near it, both clothed in leaves and underbrush, I found myself wondering what exactly there was to disturb. Still, like every place within the park, we left it as we found it, except for maybe a few newly crunched leaves on the trail.

Once we reached the escarpment ridge, the trail pretty much was the dividing line between color and not. The color side was mostly sugar maples of varying sizes. There was probably a smattering of other still-colorful trees, but it was the sugar maples that stood out.

When we emerged from the woods into our first sight of the open river valley, I was captivated by the way the Big Carp River snaked its way through the wide boggy bottom. It was a river in tranquil equilibrium with itself and its surroundings. I suspected that even up close, the flow would only be discernible by the slight angle of submerged vegetation. Where the river vanished into larger trees near the east end of the valley, I could envision it taking on the look of a north woods stream with boulders, riffles, runs, and pools. I suspected it may even hold some trout in those upper reaches.

Looking east, I recognized the features of the West Vista Overlook, even though I couldn't actually see the small opening in the trees. I could picture where we were in the scene if somebody was over there looking out at the view, and I wondered if they would notice us standing on our bare rocky protrusion.

The escarpment trail eventually passed through a mostly colorless section of oak brush. Colorless except for a few stray leathery russet oak leaves and scattered patches of low-growing sumac that were dressed in cranberry red. Looking down again into the wide boggy river valley, I thought how the scene would be perfect with one more feature—a moose. They're not in the park—yet. They tend to be roamers, though, so maybe someday the scene will be complete.

As I was still entranced, staring into the valley, a pair of swans came gracefully winging their way from the east, well below our vantage point. I don't believe I had ever watched swans flying from above. Their wing-beats looked slow and relaxed, purposeful, as they steadily worked their way toward Lake of the Clouds. Against the sodden backdrop of barren grayish trees and boggy vegetation, the swans were angelic white. Just watching them seemed to lift me above the drear. Their stark contrast faded as the birds winged their way west, through the fog of falling raindrops.

Farther west along the escarpment, sumac red was augmented by sprawling patches of ground-hugging blueberry plants, adding their own shade of red to the autumn collection.

Shortly before dropping into the saddle near the east end of Lake of the Clouds, we were treated to a glorious view of the Carp River snaking its way into the lake. To me, it was an even more dramatic view than the iconic view from the formal viewing area west of the lake. Not that the iconic view isn't beautiful. I just think the view looking west is more captivating. Then again, maybe it's just because the view looking west isn't so widely publicized and so easy to attain. Or, maybe I'm just different. Regardless, that view of the lake permeated my brain. I do have to admit, though, that it would've been even better if we weren't getting rained on at the time. Then again, maybe the atmosphere was part of what made the scene so appealing.

Shortly after that memorable view, the rain became heavy enough and consistent enough that we decided—not happily—that it was *not* the day for a fifteen-mile hike. I don't tend to take it well when my plans get washed out, but we finally decided to do a one-eighty and head back out. I thought that maybe if it quit raining before we reached the trailhead, we could just make a sharp turn to the south at the trail intersection and visit Trap Falls instead. It didn't, so we didn't.

While we were still navigating the escarpment, we saw a series of loose, low cottony clouds drifting through the valley, just above the trees. They looked like puffs of smoke, but with no campsites or cabins in that area and pretty steady rain, I ruled out woodsmoke and assumed they were just small, low-floating white clouds, adding to the sodden soberness of the day.

Despite the rain, it was still a good day for being outside, just not a good day for a long hike. So we invested the rest of the day in shorter excursions closer to the cabin, where we had the option to move our vantage point to the covered porch should the weather degrade to the point of being treacherous.

The day made me think about how dampness brings out color and details, like wetting a beach stone. The Porkies had certainly been "dipped in water", so colors and details were fully saturated. Literally. Even without bright sunshine, the landscape possessed a radiant glow. Trees and rocks had a three-dimensionality that somehow seemed exaggerated to a fourth dimension. The world was ripe for exploring.

As we roamed the familiar forest near the cabin, it was like a filter had been removed, washed away, allowing us to see the fullness of the surrounding world in its entirety. Our plans may have been rained out, but the showers had brought in a freshness that was beyond the need for rigid plans anyway.

TRAP FALLS

The first time we visited Trap Falls was in late August, on the last day of a three-day stay in the park. An evening of rain the day before ushered in humidity, which brought the biting bugs back into action. At times, we could see the moisture in the air. Even when it wasn't visible, we could certainly feel it. I've never been a fan of heat and humidity, but the bugs seemed to be thriving on it. All we knew about the falls was that someone had told Julie they were beautiful. So Julie decided that we needed to see them for ourselves. For whatever reason, I decided we should hike in from

South Boundary Road, which made for a roughly eight-mile round trip that included a non-bridge crossing of the upper Big Carp River. For the crossing, we managed to utilize some rocks and logs that other people had strategically placed in the river for just that purpose. Some teetered. Others were slippery. So Julie wasn't exactly comfortable with the crossing, but she made it without getting wet. There were a few interesting contortions and facial expressions, but no issues beyond that.

Hiking in from the south like we did, we found a long, curved chute rushing down polished orange bedrock that we at first thought was Trap Falls. It looked like the gradient and fast water continued beyond the bottom of those falls, so we continued on along the trail just to see what else there might be around the bend. As it turned out, Trap Falls was down around the bend. They were nice, as most waterfalls are, but they weren't what I would call truly beautiful. Certainly not more beautiful than the collection of Presque Isle Falls at the west end of the park.

The gradient and fast water seemed to taper off below the falls, so we decided that Trap Falls was probably the end of the show. The afternoon was sliding by rather quickly anyway, and after hiking back out, we had a three-hour drive home, so we decided to save any further explorations for our October visit.

On the way back out, I did climb up the orange rock formation along the cascading chute. Much of the rock surface was not only polished smooth, but shiny. At first, I thought it might be a quartz-based material, but after closer inspection of several locations, I realized that the elements had simply done an impressive polishing job.

During pre-trip planning for our October residency, I noticed on one of our maps that going into Trap Falls from the north didn't require crossing a river without a bridge. Accessing the area from the north would also allow us to experience a new area of the park that we hadn't explored before. So that became the plan for our October visit to the falls.

What the plan didn't include was which day we would do it. Being a relatively short hike—about six miles round trip—we figured we would fit it in whenever it looked like a good day for it. The day we had intended to venture out along the Lake Superior

Trail started out with a steady rain, so we spent some extra time around the cabin in hopes that it would let up soon. It didn't. By noon, the rain had switched to light snow, which was more promising hiking weather, but we wanted more time than just an afternoon for exploring the Superior shoreline. After a quick lunch of leftover pancakes and peanut butter, we decided that it was looking like a good opportunity to re-explore the Trap Falls area.

As we embarked on the trail from Cuyahoga Creek, the light snow was having difficulty deciding exactly what form it wanted to take—fine frozen mist, hard granules, or large wet flakes. Being a little fickle, as snow often is, it ended up just jumping around between those variations throughout the afternoon.

After crossing the Big Carp River bridge, I decided that I wanted to follow the edge of the swamp over to where the river cuts into it, then follow the river up to the falls. That way, we could experience the entire stretch of river from the swamp to the falls. We could follow the trail back out in order to see a new section of trail, too. It all sounded like a good idea. Unfortunately, ideas sometimes run amok during implementation.

Heading east through the woods along the edge of the swamp, we began encountering pockets of water, small seepages, and swampy fingers extending from the main swamp. After working our way around several of those obstacles and various land features, I noticed that the edge of the swamp was on the wrong side of us. Checking my compass, which I always carry in my pocket when I'm in the woods—or on any outdoor adventure for that matter—I found that we were indeed heading in the wrong direction. Over the years, I've had that happen on several occasions. Walking a straight line through the woods or following the edge of what looks on the map like a relatively smooth feature isn't always as easy as it sounds. Nature tends to be jumbled and a bit messy. Clear paths and easy walking don't always exist.

My intent wasn't to turn the event into a major bushwhack, so we just pointed ourselves back toward the trail and stayed the course until we found it. Then we continued on toward Trap Falls like normal hikers.

At the downstream end of the steep gradient section of the Big Carp, there are a couple of campsites near the river. We restarted our river exploration there. First, we followed the flow downstream a few hundred yards just to see what things looked like in the lower-gradient section heading toward the swamp. As I suspected, the flow soon mellowed and the river took on the appearance of a normal north woods stream without the high-gradient cascades, chutes, and falls. It looked more consistently like trout fishing water. As I often do, I made a journal note to verify that observation with a fly rod sometime in the future.

The high-gradient section of the Upper Big Carp alternates between roaring chutes, falls and caldrons, and placid, tranquil pools on a regular basis. Between two roaring falls or winding chutes is sometimes a quiet pocket that looks like a completely different river.

As we continued backtracking the flow, proportional changes in the river caught my attention. That often happens when one location looks like a large volume, both wide and relatively deep, while another nearby section looks narrow and not all that deep. It doesn't look like it can possibly be carrying the same volume of water. It seems as if part of the river somehow disappeared. I have to remind myself in those situations that velocity also comes into play. It's the flow volume that needs to balance, meaning that the cross-sectional area times the velocity needs to equate. So the much smaller looking section may be one-third of the volume of the bigger section, but it will be flowing three times as fast in order to accommodate the same flow volume. Still, it often just looks odd when a large river cross-section quickly reduces to what looks like too small of an area to carry all that water you just saw a short distance upstream.

We estimated that the entire stretch of river from the campsites up past Trap Falls—probably more than a half-mile—is an almost continuous collection of fast-water features—falls, cascades, rapids, and chutes—with those few tranquil pools mixed in for balance (and to give the fish a break). I finally understood how someone could consider the Trap Falls area to be one of the most beautiful falls in the park.

As we passed the area where the Union Spring Trail crossed the river, we both agreed that we were glad we weren't planning to cross there. The flow looked a bit too deep and fast for a safe crossing. In fact, it looked like the type of place for an unexpected swim.

I noticed that some of the falls in the Trap Falls area were log-induced and will eventually change in character as deterioration of the wood continues. Other falls were a result of underlying rock features, which are certainly more stable, but those too will change with time. The duration will just be measured in centuries instead of years.

By mid-afternoon, measurable snow was beginning to accumulate. Trees and rocks were beginning to don a veil of white. Emerging from a snowless patch of hemlocks, we noticed the snow had transitioned again from small hard granules to more fluffy irregular flakes. It wasn't looking much like October at all. We were getting back to a world dominated by the colors of white. I'm not talking about tea-stained snow from mid-winter melt moisture dripping off of beech or oak leaves still clinging to branch tips, or snow that's tinged various colors from animals doing what animals do in the woods. I'm talking about the nuances of colors from contours and textures and light intermingling across a snowy canvas. In reality, winter white isn't actually white. Snow crystals are frozen water, which is essentially clear. The collection of clear snow crystals reflects all light equally. Colors essentially cancel each other out to leave basically no color—white. Even minute changes in light or surrounding influences can alter the colors in a snow-cloaked world.

As we traversed a snow-slicked trail in this newly emerging reality, in addition to investigating Trap Falls and adjoining Big Carp River features, I found myself getting caught up in looking at and playing in some of the small tributary creeks as well. This is not uncommon for me. I have a thing for moving water. Mini rivers have the same basic features as the big rivers, just on a smaller scale. The main thing the little creeks lack is volume, which equates to power. They don't have the same mesmerizing power as their larger counterparts. But they *are* much easier and safer to investigate and play in.

Gazing into the pool below Trap Falls, a brightly colored leaf would occasionally roil to the surface as if trying to escape, only to be pulled back down again into the murky depths. Looking out into the surrounding snowy woods, I decided that we had accomplished what we came to accomplish—spend some quality time exploring the Trap Falls area of the Upper Big Carp, mentally immersing ourselves in the falls, and evaluating trout fishing possibilities. We had also done a little reconnaissance on the stretch of river down near the swampy valley bottom—not as much as I had hoped, but at least some.

So, satisfied with our progress for the afternoon, we headed north, back toward the trailhead where our adventure began and eventually to a warm cabin and hot meal.

About half-way back to the trailhead, we passed a younger-looking gal that was heading in to Trap Falls. She was wearing obviously wet running shoes with white cotton socks, which I assumed were also soaked. She was lightly dressed and didn't appear to have any additional clothes with her. The flushed look on her face and her relatively heavy breathing as she spoke to us told me that she wasn't exactly fresh. She told us that she had just done another "long" hike and was wrapping up the day with a visit to the falls. I recognized her from the Visitor Center just before we had started out on our hike, so her other hike that had her looking a little worn couldn't have actually been all that long. It was already about 5:00 p.m., with darkness not much more than an hour and a half away. I thought about making a safety-related comment as she was beginning to move on, but didn't want to insult her abilities or her judgment.

As we moved on as well and headed for the trailhead, I mentioned to Julie that I sincerely hoped that the next day we didn't hear about a rescue in the Trap Falls area. I said a short prayer, too, as we walked. Too many people go into the wilderness unprepared, thinking they're just out for a minor stroll, and end up becoming news features.

I assumed that everything worked out fine and we never heard any news to the contrary. Hopefully, as with us, her experience with Trap Falls includes vivid memories of the adventure and enthusiastic plans to return. Maybe she's thinking of some better hiking gear, too.

TRANSITION

We awoke to a cold, cloudy, mid-October morning. Depending on your location, you could experience snow, rain, or more snow. Most places received a mere dusting, but we heard of areas that got a few inches of white. As I talked to people throughout the day, it was interesting how readily most people just calmly accepted the snow, like it was just a basic fact instead of an intruder on our autumn parade. That included me.

I found myself not really taking special notice of it or mourning the fact that it would likely take a toll on the color that still remained in the forest. Maybe that means I'm truly becoming a Yooper. Or maybe it's just because the elapsed time between the last snow of spring and the first snows of fall aren't that far apart, so we mentally just don't take notice that there's a gap at all. If nothing else, the snow made me think of the fact that prime deer season was quickly approaching.

The transition from fall to winter is the most dramatic of the seasonal changes. The forest landscape changes attire and begins slowing down for its winter rest, while most forest inhabitants are gearing up and preparing for the long haul of winter. In a relatively short time, the landscape changes from a full saturation of vividly warm colors of red, amber, orange, and rust, to a sparse display of cold white, tinted with blue and lavender. With early snows, the drastic makeover often seemingly happens within a day or two. In a blink, abundant warmth falls to a chilling sparseness.

In a bit of hindsight, I thought about how it was probably good that I didn't get the artist-in-residence timing that I originally wanted, which was the prime color time of early October. If the main part of our autumn stay would have been during prime color, it would have certainly been majestically beautiful, but it would also have been extremely busy and chaotic. In addition, we would have missed the transition—that teetering on the cusp of winter while you're still reveling in autumn. Being in the park during peak color, I would have been tempted to—and probably fallen into—focusing on the big event of autumn and missed many of the little moments that we had been experiencing. So most of my timing concerns and fretting over the weather as our visit approached was for naught. With the grand event of autumn colors already waning, for most of our stay we only had the collection of little moments to focus on. In many ways, those little moments are what our focus should be on anyway. The big color event of autumn in the Porkies could probably be captured in a handful of calendar-type photographs and wouldn't even need to be described in a book. One relatively short, adjective-filled essay would probably cover it.

A few weeks before our October stay in the Porkies, I was doing some work on the Tyoga Historical Trail near my home. I remember standing under a Tyoga hemlock, trying to stay out of the rain, and thinking about our upcoming Porkies venture. I wasn't having very good thoughts. In fact, I was getting pretty disgusted with the crappy weather supposedly on tap for the upcoming week. Watching leaves falling with the rain, I was concerned for our time in the Porkies. I was pretty sure we wouldn't be seeing much, if any, color in the park by the time we finally arrived. In fact, in the mood that I was stewing in, I briefly considered throwing in the towel and just forgetting about the whole thing. Just staying home. After all, a fall color trip without colors isn't worth much. What would I write about? What would there be worth seeing? Then, I started looking around and thinking about all of the little miracles that string together to create each moment. All of the minute events that happen every second of every day, color or not, season after season. I thought of the comment by Jim Brandenburg, the popular National Geographic Magazine photographer, "It's not the big events that are important to capture. It's the little moments." Soaking there in the chilling rain, I resolved that I needed to go ahead and go to the Porkies, intent on capturing those little moments and weaving them together to create this book. After all, life is made up much more of little moments than big events. In fact, the big events that typically grab our attention are built upon a collection of little moments. The whole world, in all of its grandeur, is merely a colossal collection of those little moments that often go unnoticed.

As it turned out, by following through with our Porkies adventure we were able to experience the grand events of autumn after all, and still be there to appreciate the more subtle happenings of the flow of the seasons.

During that time of transition, I came to realize that the Porkies is one of those places where, in some ways, timing and weather don't really matter anyway. There are always interesting things to see and experience. Always adventures to plan and chase. Whether you're reveling in the big events, or quietly absorbed in the little moments, the best you can do is to simply enjoy the blessing you're living in.

PADDLING LAKE OF THE CLOUDS

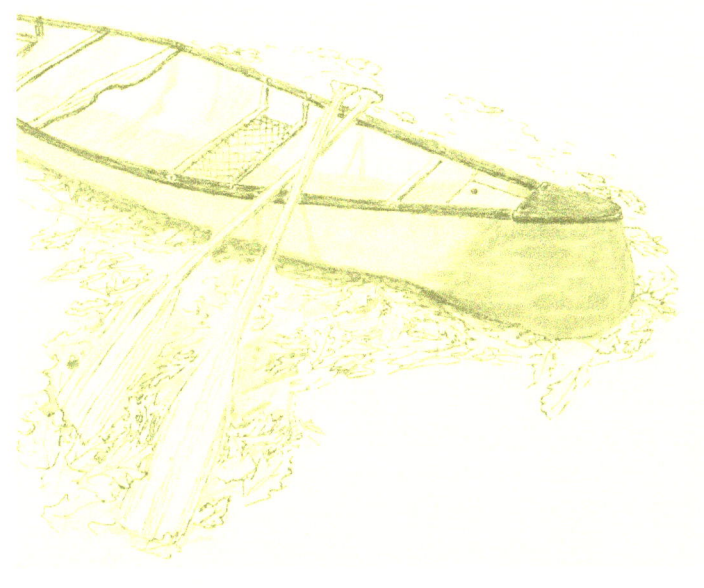

Our mid-October evening visit to Lake of the Clouds overlook was busy. Not crazy-busy as it had been earlier in the day, but busy. The sky was unmarred blue. The valley stretching east was filled with shades of amber, rust, green, and blue, the diversity of colors somehow bringing unity to the landscape. North of the lake, yellows of birch and aspen dominated. South of the lake, nearly half of the visible trees were already barren of leaves, bark-covered skeletons with a lavender hue, clawing at the sky. The scene radiated warmth, even with the cooling evening breeze. There appeared to be slight ripples on the surface of the lake, but more scrutiny revealed faint whitecaps topping each ripple. Besides taking in the Porkies' most notable view bathed in evening glow, we had come to look over details of the lake itself in preparation for our paddling excursion the next morning.

I wanted a more intimate connection with the lake than just a grand bird's-eye view. I wanted to know the lake, not just see it. I wanted to feel the freedom of gliding through its water, experiencing the grand view in the reverse direction. Our red Nova Craft canoe was perched atop our vehicle, waiting for our long-anticipated circumnavigation of the iconic lake.

We had scoped things out during a short visit back in August when we took a hike down to the water's edge and back so that I could evaluate my ability to portage our canoe into the lake. Actually, the portage *in* wasn't really much of a concern. My concern was with the portage back *out*. When we first reached the lake that August afternoon, it was quiet. Not just the lake, but the surrounding forest as well. It was just us and trees and water. For a short time, with only the voices of lake and forest, we experienced wilderness in one of the most popular places in the state.

The uphill hike out proved to be minor. I've done much worse. So, in my mind, the paddling tour was set.

As the October sun settled toward a ridge to the west, shadows began stretching across the valley and the glow began to fade. A feeling of coolness swept in. I buttoned up my jacket and we headed to our cabin for an evening fire, anticipating the dawn.

Without an alarm, other than the morning sun, it was nearly 9:00 a.m. before we were back in the overlook parking lot unstrapping our canoe. We got a few strange looks, but nobody actually made any comments. At least none that I heard. Julie carried some of our gear in a large canoe pack. I wore my daypack while carrying the boat. I normally don't wear a pack while I'm portaging the boat, so things didn't feel quite right. My portage pad kept slipping off the pack shoulder straps, which forced me to grip the canoe gunnels much tighter than usual in order to keep the boat on my shoulders. I was wearing a thin pair of gloves to provide a little insulation against the morning cold of the aluminum gunnels, which proved to be too slippery for maintaining a good grip. So, by the time we reached the point where the trail begins its descent to the lake, I was a little irritated and ready for a change. I abruptly removed the gloves and portage pad and stuffed them in my pack.

I hoisted the canoe back to my shoulders again and the portage yoke settled into place with a much better feel. We began the descent. Even though my mind was focused on my footing going down the somewhat rugged trail, somehow my imagination was already out on the lake well before we actually got there.

With Julie in the bow seat, I pushed off from shore into minor ripples that were being stirred up by a slight easterly breeze. Once we were clear of near-shore vegetation, we paddled west, into the Carp River. Just past the footbridge that is visible from the overlook, we were halted by a small beaver dam. We could have readily done a haul-over, but the water looked pretty shallow on the downstream side, so we opted to return to the open lake for much freer paddling.

The south side of the lake was still cloaked in cool shadows, but the north side was bathed in sunshine. From our vantage point in the bottom of a bowl full of wild autumn color, the view in every direction begged for a photograph. Looking up, specks of bright colors marked where trails and lookouts were located along the rocky escarpment. Early on, the colorful specks weren't very numerous, but as morning progressed, the upper escarpment was crawling with specks of brightly colored shirts and jackets.

Paddling Lake of the Clouds felt like we were in the Boundary Waters Canoe Area Wilderness in Minnesota. Bordered by craggy cliffs decorated in colorful lichens, surrounded by a north woods autumn forest, no docks protruding into the lake, sharing the lake with nobody but ducks, we could have been gliding along the shoreline of any number of Boundary Waters lakes, soaking up the solitude. I let my mind wander as we quietly paddled our way down the waterway, reveling in the moment, appreciating past experiences, and dreaming of the future.

Paddling a wilderness lake when wind and waves are mild is about as carefree of a feeling as there is. There are no dangerous currents or sweepers to beware of as there are when paddling rivers. Roots and rocks, mudholes and hills have been left behind on the trails. All that's left is the freedom to glide, letting your mind and eyes roam as they please.

Scanning our three-sixty-degree panoramic view of the basin, I don't know how many times we photographed the same basic scenes. It was hard not to, because we wanted to make sure we captured *everything* while we had the opportunity. Predictions were for a high likelihood of rain the next few days. It's not that you can't take pictures in wet conditions, we were just concerned about the resulting loss of leaves significantly altering our little world. So, with both of us wielding a camera, we gave the shutters a workout as we intermittently paddled and clicked.

For a moment, I envisioned where we were in the view from up on the escarpment. Being a part of the lake and living in the scene that most people only take pictures of, I had the surreal feeling that we were taking pictures from within a picture.

Besides exploring the lake, I had my sights set on paddling the Carp River, above the lake. I wanted to cruise through that winding Alaskan-looking waterway. But at the east end of the lake, we failed to find an actual river channel, though we searched diligently. The alders, rushes, and other vegetation did their job of guarding the entranceway. As we broke free from the drag of the rushes and were once again floating freely on the open lake, I was struck by the quiet. Not silence, but quiet. It was the lack of man-made sound—noise—that caught my attention. The light breeze still gave voice to the lake and trees, but human voices and mechanized sounds were pleasantly absent. Peaceful. Colorful specks up on the escarpment were our only reminders that other people even existed. We owned the lake, but we kept it quiet.

As we began our westward glide down the north shore, we bumped a small flock of wood ducks from shoreline cover. Apparently, our quiet approach didn't give them any comfort. One let out its mournful disapproval of our intrusion as they took flight. As they hooked south across the lake, I noticed that the sun had just begun penetrating south-shore shadows and illuminating the water's edge, giving a cheery disposition to the lake. Bringing my focus back to the nearby north shoreline, a small, lone, red-orange maple stole my attention. Even though it looked out of place in its neighborhood of rusty oaks, its seemingly random placement created a sense of harmony.

Shortly afterward, we found a spot where we could slip into shore and haul our boat out for a lunch break. We climbed twenty feet or so above the water and enjoyed our lunch snacks on a small flat protruding from the hillside, surrounded by autumn. During that short climb, I found the browned oak leaves that covered the ground to be as slippery as a thin coating of snow. The individual leaves even felt smooth and waxy, compared to the rubbery feel of maples and aspen.

Lounging there in a patch of autumn sunshine, enjoying a bit of food and some clear, cold water, felt rejuvenating. I didn't want to be anywhere else, but I knew we had to move on. Other adventures were still ahead. As we packed up, our view of the south shoreline hillside demanded a picture or two before we got back in our boat.

Once afloat, we let the breeze push us along westward as Julie continued taking pictures and I jotted notes.

The north shoreline was steep and rocky, with talus slopes descending to water's edge in some areas. Higher up, ragged cliffside rock was painted in bright greens and oranges with lichens and moss. Looking up the talus slopes at the colorful cliffs above reminded me of Colorado. Especially with the abundance of aspen and oak brush.

Along the water's edge, collections of red twig dogwood added more color to the assortment of painted leaves. Occasional pine and spruce anchored the scenery to the north woods. A quarter moon was still visible high in the northwestern sky even though it was mid-afternoon. Clouds were essentially non-existent.

Our paddle back to the access trail was leisurely while we savored the tranquility. The portage out felt leisurely as well, even though it was mostly uphill. When I paused for a few minutes at the intersection with the escarpment trail, there was a lady sitting on the bench there who had apparently just come up the same hill carrying a medium-size backpack. Based on the sweat-soaked hair around her forehead and her erratic breathing, it didn't look as if she found the climb to be at all leisurely. "You're crazy," she snapped at me, without a smile. I could tell that a pleasant retort wouldn't be appreciated. So I simply provided the smile and moved on without a comment.

A few days later, we were back on the escarpment as part of the roughly fifteen-mile Government Peak loop. From my vantage point directly above the vegetation-choked mouth where the Carp River flows into Lake of the Clouds, I was able to spot a potential route through the tangle—two, in fact. That set the stage for a revisit of the lake with our canoe the next day.

The following morning was partly sunny with sporadic flurries. I had to look close to see that the column of mercury in the thermometer was just a bit above the actual freezing mark. It had snowed just enough during the night to leave its mark on anything that didn't hold heat, like every cupped leaf on the forest floor. With mostly puffy white clouds, separated by gaps of blue, we decided to go ahead and strap the canoe on our Explorer with hopes of navigating the river above the lake.

We launched into the lake with a light westerly breeze, keeping in mind that it would be in our face on the return trip later in the day. We were on a mission, or at least I certainly was, so we paddled straight down the lake, with me practicing my J-stroke so that I would look like I knew what I was doing in case any eyes were on us from up on the escarpment.

The breeze was picking up as we began searching for the meager path through the thick vegetation. From up on the escarpment, it looked so well-defined and easy to locate. Sitting in the stern seat of a canoe buried in the reeds, it wasn't so clear. Julie said that the bow seat didn't have any better view.

We did manage to find the opening within a few minutes and began working our way eastward, using our paddles mostly as poles, pushing our way through. Within twenty yards or so it opened up into more of a navigable channel. That's where we ran into the first small beaver dam. With the structure barely showing above water, we were able to nose the front of our boat onto it where Julie was able to step out onto the woven sticks and mud. After working the canoe a little farther forward, I was able to carefully climb through the canoe and get out as well so we could slide the canoe over and into the upper water channel.

Just up around the bend, we had the opportunity to repeat the process on a slightly larger dam, still without getting ourselves wet or damaging the beaver dam. Then we paddled off into the plan I had hatched up on the escarpment the previous day.

Several wood ducks leaped into the air ahead of us without even sounding their telltale alarm. A bald eagle rode invisible currents above the edge of the escarpment, then disappeared over the ridge. Shortly after, a red-tailed hawk glided above the treetops along the north shore of the lake. Much of that side of the lake was still clothed in autumn yellow, unlike the south shore, which was primarily bare of autumn colors, looking more like early winter. We soon spotted the head of an animal moving through the water ahead of us. As it arched up out of the water to get a better look at us, we recognized the features of an otter. It quickly dove, but soon popped back up for another look just to be sure. It dove again. Its tail end arching into the river was the last sight we had of it.

Other than a few glimpses of songbirds and a few more wood ducks, that was the end of our wildlife sightings for the excursion. With all of the beaver lodges and matted-down vegetation along the banks, I fully expected to encounter a beaver or two, but that experience never came to be.

What came to be was a quiet paddle through a winding waterway, surrounded by cattails and grasses, tag alder and red twig dogwood. A little farther from the water were cedars and tamaracks in some areas. Other places, the low boggy vegetation extended out to the forest edge.

Following the river thalweg, I couldn't see bottom, so I don't know how deep the water was. Even in the lily pad-lined edges, the water was still at least a few feet deep.

When we reached the fork that we had seen from up on the escarpment the day before, we took the south branch, just to explore, even though the north branch looked like it held the most promise of passage farther upstream. Soon, we found ourselves maneuvering to turn our sixteen-foot boat around in order to follow that north branch.

Shortly after veering north, we discovered another beaver dam that wasn't visible from the cliffs above. It wasn't tall, but the opening was narrow. Narrower than our canoe, with small tag alder and dogwood guarding each side. There were branches in the water, too, keeping us from getting close enough for Julie to be able to safely step out. After debating a few possibilities, we decided it was time to turn our expedition adventure around. It was too cold and windy to chance getting wet.

It turned out for the best, because back in the main open channel the wind had picked up considerably, making paddling much more difficult. In fact, even though we were technically paddling downstream, it was much more difficult and we made slower progress that we did paddling upstream earlier. The wind had also developed a wintery sting that wasn't there earlier in the day.

As it usually is, going downstream over the small beaver dams was considerably easier than going upstream. We didn't need to search for the right channel through the thick vegetation at the river mouth, either. So, other than paddling against the wind, getting out was much easier than getting into the river.

The lake was sporting minor whitecaps, so we stopped for lunch in the shelter of the north shoreline forest as we had during our previous visit. As I re-energized, my mind wandered back through our paddling adventures. I couldn't really say if reality had lived up to what I had envisioned the experience to be or if it had exceeded my expectations. Either way, we launched back into the lake for a choppy westward ride, satisfied with another wilderness wandering.

Even though we had only done it once before, the portage back up to the overlook and parking lot felt routinely familiar, which is typical once you know what to expect. We did get a few odd looks from people, though, crossing the Lake of the Clouds overlook area on a breezy afternoon, carrying a canoe. I naturally assumed they were just envious.

WEST ESCARPMENT

Just after daylight, I looked out our cabin window at a light dusting of new snow. The last prediction we had heard was for a snowy morning and an afternoon with just a drab, cloudy sky. Our thermometer read twenty-eight degrees Fahrenheit. Those damp days that linger right around the freezing mark always seem to amplify the cold and drive it deep into your bones. It felt like a good day to lounge around the cabin, sipping tea near the fire and catching up on some reading. Looking at the calendar, though, I could see my autumn Porkies stay was winding down quickly, so a lazy cabin day wasn't an option.

We watched out the window as snow continued to fall while we ate breakfast, then we packed up for a day of adventures and headed out. Our plan was to follow the Big Carp River Trail west along the escarpment, then cross the Big Carp River and follow the Correction Line Trail to Mirror Lake. We would skirt the north side of Mirror Lake, then take the North Mirror Lake Trail back to Lake of the Clouds and the overlook. The circuit would be a little over twelve miles according to our park map.

We embarked on our journey into a partially frozen world with fresh snow, ice, water and mud, which combined to create some interesting conditions. Snow and wet leaves had frozen on the trail making quiet walking impossible. Wildlife had been out leaving tracks in the new snow, but we had no hope of actually seeing anything due to our noisy walking conditions.

Not far into our hike along the western end of the escarpment, we encountered bear tracks crossing the trail. I had suspected that recent cold, snowy weather would've sent the bears into their winter dens. Obviously, I was wrong, at least with that particular bear. The location that it was hanging around in made sense, though. High on the north side of the river valley where spring sunshine would do its work, that area would certainly warm up and thaw out much sooner than the south side of the valley or north side of the escarpment ridge. Based on similar situations I'm familiar with closer to home, the area that bear apparently chose for a den would thaw out at least two weeks earlier than some of the surrounding locations. Even though we didn't get to actually see the track-maker, just knowing wild creatures like that were out there added to the adventure of the visit and sustained the feeling that maybe there was still a chance for a glimpse.

Coyote tracks soon intersected, then followed the escarpment trail for quite a distance—probably out of habit because I doubted the trail made walking any easier for them in the current conditions. The surrounding forest was uncluttered by underbrush, providing panoramic views through the trees. Early glimpses out over the river valley showed mist-veiled views of distant features. I couldn't tell for sure if that was a result of the fine, misty snow, a light fog, or a combination of both.

Looking straight ahead as we navigated the trail, the western sky had a dismal slump to it. The fine, misty snow soon transitioned to hard granules. We had had a few recent snows, but with temperatures in the mid-thirties, they were destined for a quick melt from the start. Looking out across the valley through the veil of white, thinking about predictions for temperatures in the twenties continuing for several days, I thought, *this snow has actual potential*.

About forty-five minutes into our hike, we got our first glimpse of the Big Carp River straight below us, winding its way through the valley forest. The surface of the water looked flat and featureless, somewhat lazy. I caught just a glimpse of a large predatory bird as it launched from a nearby tree and disappeared over the ridge. The colorings reminded me of a hawk, but its movements reminded me more of an owl. I thought I briefly saw a wide, rounded head. I suspected it was a great gray owl, but I couldn't be sure.

As the trail dropped into a saddle between escarpment ridges, deer tracks joined the pathway for a short stretch, then disappeared back into the trees. Staring into the forest, my eyes strained for a sighting, while my feet followed the rolling trail as it continued west. For a hundred yards or so the trail ran along the very spine of the escarpment, with both sides of the trail falling off sharply.

Snow intensified significantly as we reached a series of open overlooks. Clouds, snow, and air churned into one. Looking straight across the relatively narrow valley, we could barely see a premonition of trees, faint gray behind a swirling curtain of white.

Soon the trail dropped down off the escarpment ridge into a large saddle and entered an extensive hemlock grove. It was like ducking under a huge canopy, sheltering us from the elements. Even though it was wide open below the canopy of green, it felt cozy. A carpet of sugar maple seedlings, still boasting yellow, hugged the ground just beyond the edge of the hemlocks. Fingers of yellow reached into the hemlock sanctuary wherever a crack in the canopy allowed.

Continuing west along the base of the escarpment with ragged cliffs towering overhead, pieces of cliff were piled alongside the trail and scattered into the forest. We had entered a different world. One the pelting white granules from the world above couldn't seem to penetrate. We quietly strolled through the stillness in a mix of hemlock and large maples, on a soft leaf-strewn trail. Used-to-be-cliff boulders lay scattered, collecting the faintest of white dustings. It felt calmly relaxing compared to our stark, daring excursion along the rocky escarpment in driving pellets of snow.

We began to hear sounds of moving water filtering through the trees. It sounded close, giving an indication that we must be closing in on our river crossing. A lone grouse flushed from high in a bare maple, which caught me by surprise because they usually explode from ground level cover. A pileated woodpecker navigated its way through the woods ahead in bursts of flight.

We reached the Big Carp River crossing just after noon, only to find the water looking a little too deep due to recent rain and snow melt. When we'd headed out from the trailhead in the morning, I knew we were either embarking on roughly a twelve-mile loop or a ten-mile out-and-back trip, depending on what we found at the crossing. It was looking like it might be an out-and-back venture.

Not wanting to give up on my plan too easily, we searched upstream for a potential crossing. Downstream was tag alders, so I figured the river would be slower and deeper. Just upstream was a tree across the river that looked promising. I made the crossing with no issues, but I knew there could still be a glitch. Julie does not do well crossing logs. I found her a sturdy walking stick to help with balance and support, but it didn't overcome her fears. She got part way across and stopped at the last place where she had branches to hang onto. Beyond that point was twenty feet of log spanning cold, deep, fast-moving water. Neither of us liked the situation, so she backed off to the safety of the riverbank.

I scouted another log spanning the river a little farther upstream, but it was smooth and slippery, which was worse. I recrossed the first tree to consult with Julie, then continued upstream in search of a potential solution to our dilemma. I found it in a relatively shallow riffle in front of the nearby campsites. The water looked to be about a foot deep. Julie's Muck boots were about sixteen inches tall, which seemed like a good match. Wading stick in hand, she carefully made the crossing and came out on the other side, dry.

I, too, was wearing sixteen-inch-high boots, but mine were L.L. Bean hunting boots, with leather uppers. They were mostly waterproof, but not quite a hundred percent. So I opted to return to the first tree for my final crossing. We ate our lunch on the south side of the river about an hour after we first arrived at the trail crossing. It took a little longer than I had hoped, but we were both dry, which in thirty-degree weather was a good thing.

A light snow soon began falling again, prompting us to move on before we chilled down too much. The first part of the Correction Line Trail was a muck slog, broken up by small creeks meandering through. Deer tracks meandered, too, keeping me on the alert again for wildlife sightings.

Eventually, we climbed out of the low area into much higher and dryer ground. The trail followed a deep ravine with a gurgling creek winding through the bottom. We dropped into the creek bottom and crossed downstream from a two-foot-tall waterfall that was confidently singing its own tune. Then the trail climbed back up into the hemlocks, where we passed a couple of bearing trees. One tree noted *50N 44W Sec 3 NW Corner*. I looked around and marveled at the original surveyors that traversed the wilderness in an effort to map it and tame its vastness. Most of us today probably can't even fathom the challenge of an undertaking like that or the fortitude that it took to accomplish it.

Snow was getting much deeper as we approached Mirror Lake. A ranger had told us that the Mirror Lake area had experienced six inches of snow a few days earlier. It was still there. Maybe plus a little more.

Before long, I was taking pictures of a colony of icicles hanging from a moss- and lichen-covered outcrop in the forest. Then the trail dropped abruptly into the Mirror Lake basin. We decided to linger along the lakeshore while we finished our lunch snacks.

Both North Mirror Lake cabins appeared to be older, full-log construction buildings which, to me, added to their appeal. I wanted to take a peek in the windows, but they both appeared to be occupied, so I simply made a note that we needed to stay there sometime for a better look. I find myself doing that sort of thing a lot.

Leaving the lake, North Mirror Lake Trail followed the flowage that I had noted several days earlier during our Government Peak hike. Beavers had made a home of it, turning the small creek into a long collection of ponds. Along the edge of one of the ponds, we came across a large decomposing hemlock trunk laying on the ground with a thoroughfare of mouse tracks emanating from it. I told Julie that I would hate to camp near it. Keeping your food and belongings safe would be nearly impossible. I had been in a situation like that before. In that case, the thoroughfare of mouse tracks had come from a pile of rocks and crossed a sandy patch along the Colorado River, at the bottom of the Grand Canyon. When I dug into my food supply to make breakfast after a night of sleeping under the stars, I found most of my food bags had holes in them and were littered with sand, leaving me with nearly a week's worth of gritty meals. So I was glad that we were just passing through.

Other than the crunch of walking on an icy trail, the world was quiet. Civilized sounds were completely absent. We hadn't seen or heard any other people since leaving Lake of the Clouds Overlook. The park was ours. It felt like a sixty-thousand-acre personal retreat.

Standing in the middle of a long beaver-swamp crossing, we were teetering on the portions of an old boardwalk that hadn't yet been submerged. Looking to the right was an extensive beaver dam holding in the swampy pond. Looking left was a snow bunting busily eating seeds from a tan goldenrod flower stem near the edge of the water. Our observations from eight feet away didn't seem to bother the little bird. It was stocking up to weather upcoming storms. A couple of quiet humans apparently were of no threat. We moved on and left our feathered friend to its business.

Coming down into the Big Carp River valley, we strode down through a long hemlock grove with a sharp ravine cut into hillside rock, listening to the little creek tumbling along the bottom of the cleft. Around, under, and over boulders, the little creek seemed carefree, flowing on toward its Carp River destination.

At the Carp River bridge, we saw the first other people since early morning. As we climbed the trail up the side of the escarpment, a flock of ten wild turkeys trotted away from us through the trees. Their presence told me that traffic on the trail must have been sparse. I took that as an indication that the fall color tour frenzy was winding down. Continuing upward, I thought about how the previous two times that I climbed that trail, I was carrying our sixteen-foot red canoe on my shoulders. I appreciated how much easier it was to be carrying my red L.L. Bean daypack instead, but I was still glad to have portaged our canoe into Lake of the Clouds. Not only was I glad that we had the experience of doing it and being able to paddle the lake, but I was thankful to physically still be able to do things like that. I was also thankful that we have places like the Porkies where adventures like that are possible.

Up top, Julie snapped a few last Lake of the Clouds overlook pictures before we headed back to the cabin. To the west was a dark sky with glowing yellow clouds. To the east was dark sky, too, just without the accent of clouds.

My initial estimate was that the day's trek would take us five or six hours. Due to a combination of mud, pictures, snow, and river-crossing issues, my watch indicated it had actually taken us about eight hours. Fortunately, the hike wasn't a race. It was an experience. It was the type of adventure that we had come to the Porkies to find.

We left the overlook feeling refreshingly tired. I had a glow of satisfaction that we had used the day well as I began dreaming and scheming about future plans.

EVENING STROLL

Late one afternoon, Julie was working on a painting at the cabin, so I decided to take a stroll along the Union River, just to get out for a walk and enjoy the north woods from the other side of the glass. I stood for a while on the bridge near the Outpost Campground, gazing intently at the river. I naturally found myself studying areas I would expect to find trout, if I were looking for trout, which I wasn't. At least I didn't think I was looking for trout. Watching water gracefully flowing through its rocky course, the last of autumn's colors fading as they swirled in pools and collected on rocks, I began missing trout season. Actually, what I was missing was trout fishing. Looking for trout, pondering their moves and motives, and admiring watery realms are thankfully always in season.

I slowly followed the Union River downstream, studying the water and surveying the surrounding forest. Absorbed in the mingling scents of woods and water, I scrutinized rocks, evaluated possible fish-holding water, and listened to the chorus of the flow. Standing on a red sandstone formation that extended into the river, I witnessed red stone being carefully and purposefully sculpted, not by a hammer and chisel, but by a drop of water and a grain of sand. Grain by grain, day by day, season by season, the red bedrock was being transformed by the river it was guiding. As with rivers not only in the north country but across the globe, the flow was continually customizing its course, giving each moment a slightly different look than the moment before or the moment yet to come.

A short way downstream from the Little Union River confluence, there was a three-foot diameter hemlock bridging the river. A monarch now at rest, awaiting its return to the ground it came forth from. For the time being, it was a walkway for squirrels, foxes, and fishers—and adventurous boys like me. It had been perched on the outside of a sharp river bend, roots providing a hollowed-out shelter for fish, branches providing cooling shade for the surrounding area. Eventually, the rushing water of a hundred or more spring melts finally undercut its supporting bank to the point where its firm support was no longer sufficient. I envisioned that a stiff north breeze may have dealt the final blow.

I crossed the bark-covered bridge and peered into the gaping hole in the bank with fractured roots protruding from its sides. I thought of how leaves and rain and the ceaseless march of time would heal that scar. New saplings will vie for the chance to take their turn reaching to the sun and filling the forest canopy opening. Oblivious to this unfolding saga, the river continued to flow, doing its appointed work. I climbed around the gap, then the river and I went our separate ways, leaving the hemlock to its journey.

Shortly after leaving the fallen hemlock behind, fading daylight prompted me to consult my wristwatch, which confirmed that it was about time to be turning my boots toward Dan's Cabin. Julie would be preparing dinner, or at least thinking about it as she wondered where I was. She would certainly know what I was up to—nothing in particular, but possibly anything. She would just be wondering where, and when I would return.

Instead of simply retracing my steps back along the river's path, I eyed a long, gradual sloping nose descending to the river from the forest floor above. It looked like an inviting path to someplace new without really leaving the neighborhood. So I followed what looked like an old trail up the nose and into the open maple woods. There, I turned south (more or less) to parallel the river back toward the cabin.

Gradually, I eased my way east, away from the river, still keeping an eye on the lip of the river valley as my guide. Farther into the open woods I ventured, looking for a familiar sight to pinpoint my location on the rough map in my head. Continually veering eastward, I lost visual contact with the river valley, but I was pretty sure I knew where it was. Nevertheless, at one point, a slight sense of uncertainty made me take a compass bearing just to convince myself I was still on the right track. As I came upon another gorge angling off from where I suspected the Union River was, I expected it to contain the Little Union. It didn't. Instead, what I found was just a series of puddles that didn't appear to have any flow at all. So I didn't know precisely where I was after all. After crossing the gully, I began angling toward where I was sure the Union River was flowing. Standing on the rim, looking down into the Union River valley, what I found was the Little Union. At least I was pretty sure it was the Little Union. Descending toward the flow for a closer look, I spotted a small patch of our cabin roof through the trees. The Little Union indeed.

I followed it home to find Julie carrying more firewood in from the tarp-covered stash in the woods. She put me to work hauling wood as she switched her focus to dinner preparation. As I was toting wood to the cabin for our evening fire, I found myself thinking that maybe I should've enjoyed my wanderings just a little longer. But then again, dinner and a fire were sounding pretty appealing, too. So I immersed myself in my appointed task and began studying the grain patterns and knotholes in each piece of firewood as I pulled it from the pile, looking forward to their conversion to cabin heat while

I later compiled my notes. As I carried the last armload to the porch, I envisioned winding down the evening by opening the woodstove door and letting the added warmth of flickering flames dance around the cabin while I relaxed in the old rocking chair.

Some days, life can be pretty complex and challenging. That day, the complexities and challenges of life were lost somewhere in the north woods.

WANDERINGS

I was mudhole-hopping along the Lake Superior Trail on my way to see Lone Rock. I wasn't really expecting anything grand or phenomenal. For some reason, the name had just jumped off the map at me, so I needed to see it. In hindsight, a lot of my wanderings seem to start that way.

Even though my sights that day were set on putting a face with a name, so to speak, for Lone Rock, I had to venture down the side trail that connects to Buckshot Cabin. The only things I really knew about the cabin were that it was on the Superior shoreline and that my daughter Megan and her husband, James, had stayed there for a few days during their honeymoon. Even though I didn't have any personal memories of the place, I suspected that a few of their memories might still be lingering around there somewhere, so I wanted to investigate.

Fortunately, I knew that the cabin was empty when I visited because I had recently encountered the two guys who had been staying there as they hiked back out to their vehicle. Knowing that I wouldn't be bothering anyone, I took the liberty of peeking in the windows to get a feel for the place. It looked comfortably simple. At one end, there was a wooden table with benches and a wooden counter nearby. The other end of the room held a couple sets of bunk beds. A small woodstove stood in the middle for heat and cooking. Everything a person really needs for a simple life in the woods.

Outside, a hedge of thimbleberries surrounded the cabin in the small clearing. Just beyond the forest edge sprawled Superior. Slowly gurgling its way past the cabin was a small creek. I envisioned that on days when wind and waves were low, keeping Superior to a whisper, the little creek could be heard sharing its soothing tune.

The quaint cabin and its north woods surroundings looked like a fitting place for starting a new life. I was glad that I stopped by, but I decided not to linger after all, being concerned that I might intrude on someone else's memories. So, I hopped across the little creek and continued on with my quest for Lone Rock.

Relying on a quick glance at my map before leaving the trailhead, I suspected that Lone Rock wasn't much farther. After traveling what seemed like a considerable distance, negotiating swampy muck-holes, I began to wonder. At one point, I decided to bushwhack my way out to the lakeshore, which was roughly two hundred yards through the thick woods, so I could get a look at the situation. Lone Rock was readily visible at what looked like a quarter of a mile to the west. I briefly considered just walking the jumbled sandstone cobble beach, but I decided the trail would be easier traveling. So, I scrambled my way back out to the trail and continued heading west.

After putting at least another half-mile of trail behind me, I finally resorted to pulling out my map to see where in the world that Lone Rock was. The map clearly showed it right in front of campsites #13 and #14. I hadn't yet made it to campsites #15 and #16, which were nearly a mile from Lone Rock. Obviously, my earlier distance estimate was flawed, which is not uncommon when you're estimating distance in a wide-open area like Superior.

After another thirty minutes of alternating between strolling through the autumn woods and squishing through autumn muck, I was standing on the shoreline, gazing out at Lone Rock. As I suspected, it wasn't anything grand or phenomenal, just a low pyramid of lichen-decorated rock, maybe a couple hundred yards off shore—you'll have to take that distance estimate for what it's worth.

A stiff breeze out of the east brought on a quick chill, so I put on my rain jacket to break the wind and tucked myself into a small cluster of beach-side cedars to eat my lunch snacks. With the sky threatening precipitation of some sort, I didn't hang around long. I *was* there long enough to notice that the campsites were pretty spartan. Along the lakeshore, though, I guess you're typically drawn to the view, not the amenities. And in this case, the view included Lone Rock, which was beginning to seem a little more special than I had originally thought. Or, maybe I was just starting to appreciate it more. Regardless, Lone Rock was no longer just a name on a map.

On a different less-than-cheery October day, my wife and I had explored another section of the Lake Superior Trail. That trek took place on the far west end of the park. What intrigued me most about the trail from the Presque Isle River mouth to the Little Carp River mouth was that it was there and we hadn't been. We decided to access the area by way of the trail to Speaker's Cabin, mainly because it represented yet another trail that didn't yet have our boot prints on it.

We arrived at the trailhead about 10:00 a.m., with snow falling or not, depending on exactly where you were at any given moment. I had to rely on our vehicle clock for the time because my watch had quit working sometime the previous evening. As we headed off down the trail, it felt a little strange knowing that we wouldn't have a good handle on the exact time the rest of the day. It shouldn't have mattered, but for some reason the planner in me just didn't like the feeling. Double-checking to make sure we had headlamps and extra batteries with us, just in case, made me feel a little better.

A quarter-mile down the trail, I heard what sounded like a robin, which caught me by surprise with all of the snow we had been experiencing lately. Even though it was only late October, I thought robins would be somewhere a little farther south than South Boundary Road. A few seconds later, though, we spotted a pair of robins on the edge of a small opening in the forest. Apparently, they were hard-core Yoopers.

The claim to fame for the area appeared to be the creeks. We crossed several on our way west to the Presque Isle River. Some were fairly substantial flows, meandering through deep and steep-sided gullies. Others were ephemeral creeks, only running when they needed to.

Every now and then, on high ground between creek crossings, we could see beyond the forest, out into the open of Superior. It looked featureless, like a gray, misty fog bank obscuring reality.

Eventually, we could hear the sounds of a serious volume of moving water. Standing on the high bank, surveying the rushing waters of the Presque Isle, I wanted to go down to the water's edge to experience the energy, but I knew that if my watch had been working, daylight would be ticking away. We still had miles to cover and sights to see, so we turned back east and began backtracking to Speaker's Cabin.

Before we went very far, a red squirrel began chastising us from its hemlock perch. For what, I didn't know, but red squirrels don't seem to need a reason anyway. We just chuckled at our antagonist's little chattering dance on the side of its hemlock safe haven and continued on through the newly-falling snow.

Snowfall steadily increased as we headed eastward. By the time we reached unfamiliar territory beyond Speaker's Cabin, our daypacks and clothes were the same wet white as the ground and surrounding forest. I was beginning to get just a bit concerned about road conditions—and eventually making it back to our cabin—but we decided to push on anyway and continue with our original plan.

The snowfall did eventually ease up, but by then there were several inches on the ground, and vegetation hanging over the trail was laden with white—until we brushed against it and the white transferred to our clothes.

As with earlier in the day, the wide variety of creeks were the main features of interest. I love moving water and exploring new creeks, but slippery, blah conditions were causing the afternoon to drag just a bit. At one point, a wide-open, deep ravine carrying the sounds of a more major flow of water had me thinking that we had reached our Little Carp destination. Something wasn't quite right, though. A quick map check showed that we were actually crossing Pinkerton Creek. Based on its size and appearance as we waded across, I put Pinkerton on my future fly fishing list as we climbed the steep bank up the other side and continued eastward.

When we finally reached the Little Carp River mouth, Superior was wavy-gray. It looked upset. Even without my watch, I knew it was getting to be late in the afternoon. Conditions weren't improving, so we didn't linger beyond a quick snack and a good drink of water.

On our way back toward the trailhead, we found where someone had recently made an adult-size snow-angel on the high bank above Pinkerton Creek. We had only passed one couple, so it must have been their doing. Julie and I agreed that we suspected it was the gal that created the snowy artwork. The guy seemed nice, but he just didn't strike me as the snow-angel type.

We also came across two different places where fresh pine marten tracks crisscrossed the trail. Even though I was watching for wildlife, as I always do, I never spotted the elusive track-maker.

Another snowy track-maker that people don't often encounter is a beaver. Seeing them out in a pond or slow-moving river isn't uncommon. Catching a beaver out in the brush or woods, felling or hauling trees, doesn't happen often. I've had the experience of seeing beavers out on solid ground a few times over the years, but what I more commonly encounter are their tracks and discarded wood chips.

One day during our January stay in the park, Julie and I were on our way to Union Spring to see the sights and acquaint ourselves with another area that we hadn't yet experienced. As we snowshoed along the untracked trail, paralleling the Union River, we came across a small grove of sugar maples, possibly twenty trees in all, that a beaver had felled and dragged away for part of its winter food supply. The belly-dragging trails meandered all around through the pale, pointed stubs. The river was probably two-hundred yards away, through a stand of mature hemlocks and a grassy riparian strip. I assumed the beaver had located the maples by smell as opposed to just randomly cruising the open woods where it would be extremely vulnerable to predators. I could envision the animal slowly waddling from tree to tree, powerfully chiseling off large maple chips around each tree trunk until the trees were sprawled horizontally in the snow, looking like a group of kids making snow-angles.

The spring itself was a dull steel-gray, same as the winter sky. A stiff breeze rippled the surface, obscuring the mysteries below. Skeletons of what were once a couple of large trees lay in the shallows, just below the water's surface, hinting at other details that we couldn't quite see. I could vaguely make out one small deeper-water pocket that looked like there may have been sandy water percolating up, but the glare of the water and our viewing angle kept its details just slightly obscured. Still, we were able to see enough to make us appreciate being there. And, I suspected that wouldn't be our only viewing of the spring.

Through our travels, I've found that if your senses are attentive, reasons to wander around in the Porkies are virtually unlimited. No matter where you go or when you go there, there are always interesting things to see and experience. Quietly navigating the Deer Yard Trail, watching the namesake whitetails going about their business of surviving. Marveling at late-season mushrooms along the Government Peak Trail with their tops curled upward, holding delicate ice crystals. Probing the depths of the Little Union River Gorge or peering in with a bird's-eye view from the gorge rim trail. Exploring ephemeral creeks, with or without the presence of water. Sniffing wildflower fragrances or savoring the sweet flavors of wild berries. In the Porkies, there are always good reasons for wandering.

Unfortunately, many people we've seen in the Porkies appear to be missing quite a bit of what the park has to offer. They're only looking for the big events and iconic views. To see a few sights and take a few pictures to show friends or post on Facebook or Instagram, or whatever is the latest thing to do. They're here and gone again, never really experiencing the park, not realizing that most of the best views in the park are not visible from a parking lot or roadside turn-off. It takes foot-power, and maybe even a little sweat, to gain access.

I've also noticed numerous people listening to music as they walk the trails. Some have their phone or whatever device blaring from their pocket, letting it disturb the peacefulness of everyone and everything around. Others at least put earbuds in and keep their tunes to themselves.

Either way, they're missing part of the park, part of the experience. It's like watching a movie without the sound. They're present, but not completely. They miss the benefits of honestly being immersed in their surroundings. The musical notes of nearby songbirds, a breeze through the trees, the cry of a hawk, the cackle of a pileated woodpecker, and the faint music of moving water calling through the forest are all lost to the strangling grip of civilization. Electronic devices have worked their way so deeply into our lives that some people can't even fathom functioning without them. They're shocked to find that their cell phone doesn't work in the middle of the wilderness, and they're lost—sometimes literally—when the charge runs out on their GPS device.

They just can't seem to let themselves break free of the man-made world. It still holds them hostage, even in the wilderness. Maybe they don't realize what they're missing. Maybe they're afraid to let go of civilization and fully step into the wilds. Maybe they're so far removed from the natural world that partial reconnection is all they can handle. True immersion would be somewhat of an overdose for them.

Regardless of the reason—good, bad, or indifferent—they're missing part of the park. In fact, they're missing a *big* part of the experience.

It seems that some people want to get out and get away in the real world without disconnecting from their virtual world. That brings up the question that if you don't disconnect from the virtual world, can you ever truly connect (or reconnect) with the reality of the natural world? To me, the answer is *no*. Of course, that's a strongly biased opinion because I'm on the opposite end of the spectrum. I spend very little time in the virtual world, only dabbling in it when I absolutely need to. Even then, I'm always looking for an opportunity to ditch it and get back to reality.

That being said, the natural world that was created with us in mind, to provide for our needs and fuel our imaginations, is always out there, waiting for us to return. Whether we're completely tuned in and immersed in that natural reality or just taking a quick peek without fully diving in, endless opportunities are always out there.

In the Porkies, as with wild places across the country, the best way to connect with those opportunities and find your way home, is to simply pick a place and begin your wanderings.

Walking into Winter

We awoke to three inches of wet snow clinging to what was a world of amber and orange the evening before. Colors were technically still present but certainly not bright. As a result of the overnight snowy breeze, in some areas the ground was a literal mix of leaves and snow. The snow had stopped, at least for the time being, but what was left of the leaves continued to trickle down.

We decided to go up onto the east end of the escarpment to take in snowy views of the Carp River and Lake of the Clouds, then transition to the Overlook Trail to see what West Vista looked like cloaked in white. When we headed out mid-morning, new snow was still on hold, but existing snow was falling from the trees. Even with the fresh coat of white mingling with bright sugar maple and aspen leaves, the world was sullen-grey due to an overcast sky and hints of misty fog hanging here and there. With that same area having been brilliant amber just a few days ago, it looked like autumn color had met its match during the night. Heavy, wet snow, cold, and a little breeze had combined to take their toll on fall.

Part way up our escarpment climb, not much past the old Cuyahoga Mine site, pine marten tracks joined the trail. It looked like mice and squirrels had been busy already, too, which likely explained the marten tracks. The tree-climbing hunter was no doubt on the prowl. Not that I dislike mice and squirrels—well, actually, I do have an issue with mice from time to time—but I hoped my fellow hunter had a successful morning and ate well.

Gaining elevation, I was surprised to see that there were still some golden yellow leaves attached to branches, but there had been a noticeable toll. The remaining colors, besides white, were primarily due to sheltered maples and die-hard oaks.

As we climbed, dwindling leaves and the lingering scent of autumn reminded me of family gatherings at our log cabin near Tahquamenon Falls. We always spend time there in the fall and my mind began making the journey once again. I've noticed that I tend to have a problem staying in the moment when I'm hiking, and sometimes even when I'm seriously exploring and trying to stay focused. I have so many memories stashed in the back of my mind from previous adventures that things in the present keep triggering recollections from the past, and my thoughts tend to seriously wander. I also tend to be a dreamer and a planner, so present sights and experiences cause me to hatch new plans for future adventures, then my mind starts envisioning those activities. With my mind so easily jumping forward and backward, I sometimes find it extremely difficult to keep myself grounded in the present moment so that I don't miss anything in the now. In fact, there have been numerous times that I've walked right up on wildlife without noticing them because my head was sidetracked somewhere else.

As we neared the first rocky escarpment overlook, I got strong whiffs of a slightly pungent herbal aroma. I've noticed the same aroma in many places, not just in the Porkies. I believe it's simply the damp woods being steeped, being cold-brewed into a woodland tea of sorts. I've yet to pinpoint a specific source for the smell, but it does often seem to be associated with oak brush. Doing the research to actually figure it out just hasn't become a priority yet.

The trail turned out to be a perfect blend of mud and snow for maximum slipperiness. There was just enough snow to hide what you were stepping on without providing enough depth to give you any traction. The first few snows of the season often tend to be like that.

Standing in the open escarpment overlooks, gazing out across the valley and beyond, the world looked cold and forbidding. Yet, there was a certain allure. It looked like a world of mysteries that needed to be investigated. I found myself wanting to be out there to see things close-up. To make those unknowns known.

A whole new world had been born during the night. Autumn had made another big step toward winter. The autumn-stealing snow many of us had been dreading for a variety of reasons was no longer a near-future possibility or threat. It was here, transforming the world overnight. This new world wasn't necessarily any better or worse than the world of yesterday, just different. Technically, it wasn't really winter yet, but based on appearance, it wasn't really autumn anymore either. At least not at the moment.

I found myself thinking of deer hunting in that new white world. Firearm season was still a few weeks away, but that's where I found my mind wandering off to as we roamed the open, snowy woods. We were blessed to be the first ones up on the east end of the escarpment that morning, leaving tracks in an untracked world. Well, at least untracked by other people. The world was ours to marvel at and ponder. We took plenty of pictures, knowing most of them wouldn't even come close to capturing our feelings or the mood of the moment. Still, we took them anyway, hoping for the best.

Soon, a biting west breeze replaced the initial morning calm. We decided it was time to retreat to the Overlook Trail and West Vista. We knew the chilling breeze would find us there, too, but at least we would have some time of respite in the forest between and generate another dose of heat with the impending climb.

During our climb to West Vista, up the north side of the Overlook Loop, we passed through a variety of hemlock groves. With virtually no snow in them, the hemlock groves felt especially dark and secretive. I also noticed that after the past several days of negotiating mucky trails, the mudholes had ceased to be a dreaded obstacle and had simply become an accepted fact. They're the reason we typically wear tall boots instead of just hiking shoes—or in my younger days, old running shoes. My new outlook tends to be that if our main goal was an easy-going stroll, then we would need to just find a sidewalk somewhere. Our natural world has mud and muck and watery holes with slippery rocks and logs. In a way, it's part of what makes the adventure. It's the price of admission for the sights we see and the experiences we're blessed to have.

Thimbleberry leaves that just the day before looked like big yellowy-green hands waving along the trail now hung soft and wrinkled, looking a little worse for wear. They reminded me now of a limp handshake.

As we came up to higher elevations, it felt like we had walked into January again. Snow was the deepest we had seen yet, causing trailside vegetation to hang into the trail. We stopped for lunch at the edge of a small hemlock grove where we could look out into winter while still being sheltered in autumn. Sheltered at least until a breeze shook some winter on us from the branches.

Coming up to West Vista looked nothing like when we were there just ten days before. That time, we climbed one of the ski hill runs —where I got bit by a pesky mosquito—and came in from the back side. The day had been cloudless, sunny and warm, verging on hot. Our fogged-in view from January hadn't prepared us for the view we walked into that afternoon. My first sight of the line of escarpment mountains, with the wide valley and Carp River winding through it, reminded me of Alaska. I fully expected to see a moose stroll into view out in the river valley. We could just barely see the east end of Lake of the Clouds. Just a slight glimpse. North of the escarpment ridges, Superior hazily rested. Based on shape and relative location with respect to Lake of the Clouds, I was pretty sure I recognized the primary lake overlook viewing area, but it was too far off to see the colorful specks of visitors crawling around on it. During that earlier visit, I found myself thinking about how much ground there was needing to be explored between West Vista and Lake of the Clouds. I was glad that we had finally done some of that exploring.

Looking into the distance from West Vista again still reminded me of a scene we may have witnessed in Alaska. Now so even more with snow and a slight haze making distant features appear even more distant than they really were and adding to the feeling of vastness. Unlike when we were there in January, in October, we could actually see those distant features and appreciate the vastness of the area.

As with our escarpment views earlier in the day, the chilling west breeze, now hitting us directly in the face, cut our viewing short. We retreated once again to forest shelter, looking ahead to adventures yet to come. Our hike down the south side of the trail loop was much more gradual than some of the sections we came up on the north side of the loop. With slippery conditions, though, our direction of travel worked out well. I would much rather climb up steep, slippery trails than go down them. Going down steep, slippery trails tends to produce more ungraceful moments, some of which can even degrade to incidents. I prefer to avoid incidents.

Winter faded as we made the descent. Instead of a snow-covered world accented with a smattering of colored leaves, it looked more like autumn with the minor setback of a brief dusting of snow. There was still hope that the glowing warmth of autumn would soon return. In the meantime, we made our way back to the glowing warmth of an autumn evening fire.

VIEWS

Mention the Porkies and most people think of Lake of the Clouds. More specifically, they think of the view looking east from the main escarpment overlook. The cliff-lined lake with the Big Carp River valley extending eastward is certainly a noteworthy view, especially when it's draped in the warmth of autumn colors. That's the view that people flock to the park to see. It's the view that everyone leaves with a picture or two of in their camera—or these days, on their phone.

I, too, have a number of pictures of that view from many slightly different orientations, angles, and vantage points, both in print and pixels. When it comes to vista-type, calendar-worthy pictures, though, the Porkies have much more to offer beyond that one iconic snapshot. All along the escarpment, both east and west of the formal Lake of the Clouds overlook, are picture-worthy views. My absolute favorite view from the escarpment is from just east of the break in the cliff, near the east end of Lake of the Clouds. The Big Carp River winds its way through the secluded valley below before it enters the east end of the lake. The view looking west from your perch on the escarpment, with the serpentine river gently filtering into the lake that's bordered by rocky palisades, and a range of rugged hills fading into the distance, rivals any view in the state. At least in my mind it does.

Moving your vantage point farther east, to the West Vista Overlook, is another Porkies view to write home about. A majority of the Big Carp River valley stretches west in front of you, with the east end of Lake of the Clouds barely visible in the distance. That view gives me the feeling of looking into the vast mysteries of the wilderness. I yearn to be out there in that view, to change those wilderness mysteries into experiences. In fact, that view, during our January visit, was part of the impetus for my plan to paddle Lake of the Clouds and the Upper Big Carp River Valley. I wanted to live in that panoramic picture stretching across the unknown in front of West Vista.

Even farther east is the ski hill. There, whether you gain the summit by riding the chairlift during winter operation, or under your own power any time of year, it gives the feeling of being somewhere above the ordinary. You get the opportunity to glimpse a broader scope of reality than lower elevations afford. The openness of the ski runs allows you to see details at distances much farther than most anyplace else in the park. Once, when we had climbed the hill during the off-season, we watched a whitetail doe and her grown fawn calmly grazing across one of the slopes a few hundred yards below us. They were oblivious to the fact that they had an audience.

Another memorable view in my Porkies recollections is from the eastern end of the Lake Superior Trail. As I stepped out onto a rocky ridge of outcroppings and oak brush, Superior was in the distance, beyond the immediate forest, stretching out into forever. The world was quiet, except for Superior's faint murmurings drifting across the landscape. As I stood there absorbed in the vastness, thinking far-off thoughts, a slight breeze arose, temporarily blotting out Superior's voice. The chattering of a nearby chickadee brought me back to the immediate, leaving the vastness to ponder another time.

Superior views directly from the water's edge are different. The sense of vastness is still there, to a certain degree, but not to the extent of an elevated view of the lake. From a shoreline vantage point, what usually strikes me, at least on calm days, is the vastness of its secrets. I wonder at and speculate about its benthic features and the relics that have collected there over the expanse of time. Thoughts of its living inhabitants swim through my mind.

On less-than-calm days, up-close views of the Big Lake roar of raw power. Pent-up energy of wind and waves drives emotions ranging from awe to fear, as Superior rearranges its shoreline and adds to its collection of relics. On those days, even though the focus is usually on the pounding of nearby waves, the far-off horizon is still periodically in view, beckoning your thoughts to wander.

When I think of truly panoramic Porkies views, though, I can't help but think of Summit Peak. At 1,958 feet above sea level, it's already the highest point in the park. The rustic wooden observation tower perched atop the peak amplifies the visibility even more. Rising up out of the forest and having the ability to look all around brings a sense of wide-open freedom. Even though I couldn't really see any one particular feature of the park from there, I felt like I was looking at everything in the park. It was like being in a hot-air balloon, surveying the expanse of the Porkies.

That's the beauty of wide-open views. We can see beyond ourselves, beyond the immediate. We begin to grasp the vastness of the world around us and start to understand that there is much more to life than what we experience at any one location or at any one moment. We begin to sense that there is much more out there than we will ever see or experience firsthand. The world we live in is much more unknown than known.

Views like those sometimes make me wonder what I'm missing by not being somewhere else. But then again, if I was somewhere else, then I would be missing what was happening where I'm at. I've found that I can't think about it too much or it can give me a headache. I just have to accept the fact that there is a lot of exploring to do, so I should never be bored.

Up close and personal encounters with the landscape often spawn an adventurous scheme or two in my head. Expansive views, though, usually hatch an entire school of dreams. Some of those plans and dreams are relatively ordinary and tame. Others can be as unique and wild as the wide-open landscape that generated them. It just depends on your view.

Wish List

So, what about that head full of dreams and plans that I mentioned earlier? Well, as of the writing of this book, most of those dreams and schemes are still on my wish list. The list itself is not all that long. It's manageable. Accomplishing all of the items on the list, well, that'll take some doing—and some time. While I'm working on planning those adventures to possibly fill the pages of a second Porkies book, I'll at least share the list that's bouncing around in my head and spilling out into notes on my park maps.

One of the obvious goals is to finish hiking all of the trails in the park. There are not many left to hike for the first time, but enough to be worth noting. There are a few miles of the Lake Superior Trail between Lone Rock and the Big Carp River mouth that my boots haven't trod yet. There are also a few miles of the Big Carp River Trail from the Correction Line Trail to the river mouth that still need exploring, too. The trails around Lily Pond are still unknown to me, as is the Pinkerton Trail. Overall, we're only talking about roughly seventeen miles of hiking in order to finish covering all of the black trail lines on my Porkies map—not really a major challenge.

The blue lines are a different story. When it comes to fishing all of the "fishable" rivers and creeks in the park, I've barely begun. There is probably no good way to figure exactly how many stream-miles we're talking about, but it's certainly many times the number of stream-miles that my fly rod and I have fished so far. With all of the blue lines showing on park maps, and considering the fact that fishable water changes season to season, as well as year to year, the remainder of my lifetime may not be long enough to actually accomplish this dream. I suppose, though, being that most, if not all, of the streams in the Porkies eventually feed into Lake Superior, that I could just fish Superior and technically be fishing all of the streams at the same time. That being said, checking something major off of your wish list based on a technicality—especially one that's a stretch—doesn't really count. After all, my real goal here isn't just fishing the water and hopefully catching some trout. The underlying goal and driver of this dream is to explore the streams and the geography that cradles them.

Thinking about my earlier comment on how the rivers and creeks are constantly changing, I guess that I can never truly say that I have explored them all, no matter how much time I spend fishing in the Porkies. So exploring all of the Porkies streams with my fly rod in hand is probably one of those dreams that you can happily chase, knowing that you will never actually catch it.

While I'm talking streams, this is probably a good place to mention Trap Falls. Of course, I've experienced Trap Falls before, but not in the prime of winter. I want to experience the Trap Falls area of the Upper Big Carp River during its winter transition. Like when we witnessed Nonesuch Falls and the Little Iron River going through the transformation to its winter state of suspended animation, I want to experience that at Trap Falls. I want to see that stretch of rushing water slowly solidifying, from the first delicate icicles and crystal-covered rocks, to the amber-tinted shell that eventually bridges its flow. I want to hear its muffled voice from within its icy armor while the flow awaits its spring unleashing.

Sometime, I would also like to meet that flow, and the flow of all of the Porkies streams, as they fan out into the Big Lake. I want to kayak the entire Porkies Superior shoreline.

At roughly twenty-six miles, it's certainly not a daunting task. From a safety standpoint, the shoreline isn't guarded by cliffs that would keep you from exiting the water if wind and waves become menacing. There may not be easy exits everywhere, but accessing solid-ground shelter is possible. Having kayaks designed for big water—which we do—would certainly be advisable. So the major hurdle to this goal is being in the park and ready to go when a day or two window of pleasant paddling conditions opens up. I know of experienced paddlers with sea-worthy kayaks that have paddled Superior in the midst of six-to-eight-foot waves, but that's not part of my dream. I would rather spend a day or two, maybe even three, experiencing the Porkies shoreline from a watery vantage point in a more relaxed scenario. Fighting for my life while I'm trying to reach my intended take-out destination is not part of my dream.

These days, if you want to spread the experience over multiple days, being able to reserve a campsite or two during your window of paddleable-water can also be an issue. Still, it all basically comes down to planning and logistics. This venture is near the top of my Porkies wish list, so I suspect it will happen. It's just a matter of when I take the time and figure out all of the logistics.

For a much more easily planned adventure, I want to watch a sunrise from Summit Peak. I envision seeing the light of a new day cautiously creeping in over the eastern horizon from that expansive bird's-eye view to be worthy of a bucket list.

The same goes for watching a flaming sunset from the West Vista Overlook. I envision the western sky painted in varying and mingling shades of red, orange, and yellow, while the Big Carp River valley and surrounding ridges descend through the gray-scale until they're nearly black against the backdrop of an evening sky.

Of course, in both cases, the nuances of the sky will depend on the conditions of the day, so these adventures will need to be repeated at least a few times to get the full benefit of the experience.

Both of these adventures would also involve a headlamp-lighted hike in the dark. That in itself would be an interesting undertaking, but it's not part of my dream. Now that I think of it, though, an adventurous dream enabler like a headlamp hike would magnify the uniqueness of those sunrise and sunset experiences. So, even though the hikes by headlamp may not be part of my original dream, they're an integral part of making things happen and would enhance the experiences to an even higher level of special. That automatically makes the hikes not only a necessary part of the plan but an inviting part of the experience.

Getting back to big—maybe even audacious—dreams, all of the real estate between trails pulls at my brain every time I look at a map. I want to somehow explore those expanses between the trails to at least glimpse the Porkies that only its full-time wild residents normally experience. When I hike the trails, I'm constantly scanning the surrounding forest and wondering what's beyond what I can see. Perched up on the overlooks, I want to see for myself what is in those trees spreading out below me. I want to climb those hills and ridges rising in the distance to see what other dreams they may ignite.

Sometimes I wonder if this wish list even has an end. Then I come to the realization that there *will* ultimately be an end to it. The end of the list, though, won't be due to a lack of dreams. It'll be due to the lack of a further need for dreams, when my seemingly infinite list of unknowns here on earth become known. Until then, regardless of miles hiked or paddled or fished, my wish list of adventures continues to grow.

Parting Thoughts

It occurred to me during one of our many park-wide hikes that in addition to grand scenery like the Presque Isle River and Lake of the Clouds, the Porkies are full of small surprises. "Little moments," as National Geographic photographer Jim Brandenburg once noted. Little moments to capture our imagination and our heart. Every second is a new moment. Faint flutterings of soft snowflakes or dancing leaves. An eye-catching ripple or swirl in swift water. A thin sheet of tannin water flowing over a hidden ledge of sandstone or shale. A lone flower boldly defying the elements. A leaf, freshly painted by a grand artist. Delicate crystalline ice formations catching morning rays. Unexpected encounters with wildlife great and small.

JOHN HIGHLEN

An intriguing scent drifting on a soft breeze. Superior quietly breathing, without even moving a grain of sand. The fragrantly sweet taste of wild berries. The barely-audible tinkling of a trickle of water through the forest. Towering trees. Quiet solitude. Our own thoughts, emerging from that moment, enhancing our life.

This vast collection of little moments, mingled with the grand scenery, all blend together into our Porkies experience. Somewhere in the recesses of our consciousness, or maybe deeper yet, it's why we come to the Porkies. Maybe more importantly, it's why we come back.

ABOUT THE AUTHOR

For more than five decades John Highlen has been enjoying pursuits such as hiking, hunting, fishing, backpacking, canoeing, kayaking, exploring, and climbing, as well as many others. These years spent absorbed in the outdoors, experiencing nature from numerous perspectives, has given him a deep appreciation of and respect for our natural world. As a degreed mechanical engineer, John is able to recognize and understand the details of what he sees and how those details work together in the grand scheme. Overall, this eclectic blend of skills and experience allows him to see and interpret the natural world through a unique set of eyes. John strives to use those skills and experience in his writing to help connect readers with the natural world everyone is meant to be a part of and all of the intrinsic benefits that flow from that connection. In 2016, John was blessed to be able to turn his attention full-time to outdoor adventures, writing, volunteering for conservation organizations and being the support crew for his wife, Julie's, art studio.

In 2019, John had the privilege of being an artist-in-residence with the *Listening Point Foundation*, in Ely Minnesota. There, he focused his writings on Sigurd Olson's beloved Listening Point and the nearby Boundary Waters Canoe Area Wilderness.

In 2020, He and Julie were each blessed with an artist-in-residence with the *Friends of the Porkies*. Having an opportunity to live a simple life in the Porkies wilderness for more than a month that year, focusing on interpreting his outdoors experiences, helped solidify John's desire to write.

John and his wife enjoy living in Deerton, Michigan, in a home surrounded by woods, less than ten minutes from the wonders of Lake Superior. From this vantage point, they paint the wilds of the north woods and waters to share nature's inspiration with others—Julie with brush and canvas, John with pen and paper.

www.ingramcontent.com/pod-product-compliance
Lightning Source LLC
Chambersburg PA
CBHW020258030426
42336CB00010B/818